May Day at Yale, 1970: Recollections

This book comes from firsthand experiences, both in words and in pictures. It offers a partial record of a community and an institution coming together to accommodate an event while deflecting its potential violence. The history of the New Haven Green bridges over four centuries. It has served as a place for worship, grazing cattle, staging revolutions, hanging the unlawful, and for hosting various causes and campaigns.

On the day before and on May Day of 1970, Yale University and New Haven prepared to host an agitated congregation of young civil rights activists with a diverse list of causes, but focused mainly on freeing Bobby Seale, the Black Panther leader. This book gives a glimpse of that diversity; diverse in cause, attitude, and dress. More important, it shows a common decency that defined the day. Yale and New Haven could be proud of avoiding any real violence and bloodshed.

Like an archeological record, this book not only documents the New Haven Green on that one day, but marks a broader shift in direction for the country at large. For those who remember being there, it seems painfully near. For later generations, it is likely a remote abstraction.

JTH

MAYDAY

ORSON WELLES
WED JUNE 10
2:30 & 3:00 FREE

May Day at Yale, 1970 : Recollections

The Trial of Bobby Seale and the Black Panthers

Narrative by Henry "Sam" Chauncey

with photographs by

John T. Hill and Thomas Strong

taken before and during the 1970

May Day demonstration in New Haven

supporting Bobby Seale and the Black Panthers

Introduction by Henry Louis Gates, Jr.

Poster for a May Day film screening
at the Orson Welles Theater
in Cambridge, Massachusetts.

Prospecta Press, 2016

Published by

Prospecta Press

P.O. Box 3131

Westport, CT 06880

www.prospectapress.com

(203) 571-0781

info@prospectapress.com

Printed in China

Hardcover ISBN 978-1-63226-021-5

eBook ISBN 978-1-63226-022-2

Paperback ISBN 978-1-63226-066-6

First hardcover printing: March 2015

Paperback reprinted: March 2016

eBook published December 2015

Bobby Seale was born in 1936 in Dallas, Texas. He and his family lived in poverty for a number of years.

Seale and Huey P. Newton founded the Black Panther Party in 1965 as an organization for black and white people who wanted to fight what they saw as a racist society. Seale was a defendant in two trials: one as a result of the unrest at the 1968 Democratic convention and the other, the trial discussed in this book. Seale was not convicted in either trial.

Today he lectures around the country and is the author of *Seize the Time: The Story of the Black Panther Party and Huey P. Newton.*

Tom Strong

Introduction   *Henry Louis Gates, Jr.*

On the eve of May Day, 1970, a nation weary of a war increasingly perceived as immoral and rocked by ongoing racial tensions still raw from the assassination of Martin Luther King, Jr., awaited Armageddon in perhaps the most unlikely place of all: on the campus of Yale University in downtown New Haven, Connecticut, where I was a sophomore. Our expectations were that a mass demonstration of college students, black and left-wing radicals, and perennial "outside agitators" would sweep over the Green in protest over the jailing and unfair trial of two Black Panther Party leaders accused of conspiring to murder one of their own. Many thought it was the government that should have been on trial for manipulating the case to break the Panthers' backs, while a far dirtier operation was underway in Vietnam. That no lives were lost by the following sunset was a miracle. Actually, much of the credit goes to the legendary president of Yale University, Kingman Brewster, and his special assistant, Henry "Sam" Chauncey, and to four black student leaders, Ralph Dawson, Glenn De Chabert, William F. Farley, Jr., and Kurt Schmoke, who answered the "mayday" call for peace that May the 1st, and in doing so, helped defuse what easily could have been "Kent State" before the real tragedy of the murder of protesting students at Kent State devastated the country three days later.

The facts are expertly reported in Paul Bass and Douglas W. Rae's definitive book, *Murder in the Model City: The Black Panthers, Yale, and the Redemption of a Killer* (Basic Books, 2006). The murder of the 19-year-old Black Panther Alex Rackley in New Haven on May 20, 1969, resulted in the arrests of two Black Panther leaders, Ericka Huggins and Bobby Seale (in addition to the killers, also Panthers), as part of the federal government's determination to crack down on the party's growing media presence and popularity. By the following spring of 1970, the remaining Panther leadership set their sights on New Haven as the new ground zero in their war against "the system," capitalism, and "white oppression." [1] Monitoring the situation at Yale was President Brewster and, in Washington, President Richard Nixon and FBI Director J. Edgar Hoover, neither of the latter exactly on cozy terms with Black America.

The escalation began on April 14, 1970, when black area high school students, rebuffed at the local courthouse, took their frustrations out on the Chapel Square Mall. The next day's reaction witnessed further violence at Harvard University in Cambridge, Massachusetts, when the administration there locked its gates on 1,500 protesters massing in the streets with nowhere to go but the hospital. In response, the Youth International Party (Yippie) leader Abbie Hoffman announced that the Movement's next step would be Mother Yale, as we affectionately nicknamed the institution that we had come to love. [2]

To head off Hoffman, President Brewster, in a stunningly clever move, characteristic of the tenor of his presidency, conferred privately with Harvard point man, the law professor Archibald Cox (of future Watergate fame), who warned Brewster not to make the same mistake Harvard had made in locking down the campus. [3] The fabled Harvard-Yale rivalry aside, this was a classic example of two brilliant men, both broadly liberal in their sensibilities and both national leaders, seeking to avert another campus disaster, one that would have enormously harmful ramifications throughout the academy, spilling over into the larger society outside, especially since both institutions had only recently begun to implement affirmative action admission policies that had led to the admission of the largest number of black students in the freshman class at either institution.

As May Day approached, Black Panther organizer Doug Miranda exhorted Yale students to burn their campus down in protest of Bobby Seale's capture: "You ought to get some guns, and go and get Chairman Bobby out of jail!" [4] His hope was to spark a more protracted strike, even if that meant risking the lives of my fellow Yalies. "That Panther and that Bulldog gonna move together!" Miranda shouted to thunderous applause at Battell Chapel on April 19—the anniversary of the Battle of Lexington and Concord, for what it's worth. [5] Soon, t-shirts with the two animals, one black, the other white and blue, peppered the campus. Stepping forward to lead the student committee was my friend, Bill Farley, who would be selected as a Rhodes Scholar in his senior year (Class of 1972). Farley, along with Ralph Dawson (Class of 1971), Moderator of The Black Student Alliance at Yale (BSAY), Glenn De Chabert (Class of 1970), and Kurt Schmoke (Class of 1971), who would be chosen as a Rhodes Scholar the year before Farley and would go on to be elected the first African American mayor of Baltimore in 1987, made the critical decision to open a back channel to President Brewster, even as Farley publicly warned of his plans to help shut Yale down. I remember when that decision was made: De Chabert, during an emergency meeting of the BSAY, said that he had come to the realization that the Panthers actually wanted to "heighten the contradictions," as the left-wing saying went, by showing the country that even white, privileged Yalies could be the victims of the police brutality sure to ensue in the chaotic aftermath of the May Day rally. The BSAY would cooperate with Kingman, he said, to keep that from happening.

All of a sudden, it was the Panthers who had to be controlled. Supported, yes; but also their activities and influence controlled. And that was going to take some deft footwork. We became so alarmed, and frankly frightened, by the escalating threats that we attempted to force the black female members of BSAY to seek protection during the rally within the formidable walls of the Scroll and Key secret society, much against their wishes.

Brewster, Dawson, De Chabert, Farley, and Schmoke were natural allies: each a strong leader, each charismatic, each as strongly attached to his ethnic identity as he was attached to Yale. Black, and Blue. And while my three friends and fellow black students were, to a person, left of center and cultural nationalists, they never, even once, considered violence or anarchy a viable option for the black community, especially the black community at Yale. "Black and Blue" was our generation's motto. And these three guys wanted to lead America, not destroy it. What's more, nobody in their right mind wanted to see anyone killed in the process of protesting the miscarriage of justice that was occurring in the New Haven courthouse, or the Vietnam War. Only mad or desperate women or men embraced that option, and Dawson, Farley, De Chabert, and Schmoke were anything but mad: each had come to Yale to transform the system from within, not to tear it down. And each found in Kingman Brewster—most famous before the strike, I think, for his annual speech to the freshmen welcoming them to New Haven as this year's cohort of Yale's "One Thousand Male Leaders"— a model of how the power elite, at least as Brewster defined and embodied it, was dedicated to integrating the American power structure and simultaneously perpetuating the ruling class by diversifying it with "natural aristocrats," as the saying went. And if ever this curious phrase applied to four born leaders, it was to Dawson, De Chabert, Farley, and Schmoke.

April ended with the worst boiling over: at a mass meeting on the 21st before a standing-room-only crowd at Yale's Ingalls Rink, Black Panther David Hilliard (just that day freed from jail) was boldly challenging the crowd of thousands of our fellow students to "off the pigs," when an architecture student, deranged enough to jump on the podium in the middle of Hilliard's speech, was beaten by Hilliard's security, much to the horror of all of us Yalies. Suddenly, "the Revolution" wasn't just a phrase any longer; human beings like us were as vulnerable to violence as any inner-city resident being victimized by the police. "Fuck you! All power to all those except those who want to act like a bunch of goddamn racists," Hilliard exclaimed, as he coaxed the crowd to recover from the stomping

of that student, who ultimately was allowed to speak.[6] We couldn't tell if this guy's incoherent mumblings were a sign that he had been imbalanced before he jumped on the platform, or a sign of how badly he had been beaten by Hilliard's bodyguards. But the effect of that beating was terrifying, and I think it contributed considerably to our determination to protect this university of which we found ourselves a vital part and which, we suddenly realized, we had come to love.

With his options vanishing, President Brewster heeded Archibald Cox's advice: after making a show of defiance, he "relented" by agreeing to keep Yale's gates open on May Day.[7] You might call it Brewster's safety-valve plan. It included his decision to announce at the next Yale faculty meeting on the 23rd that academic "expectations" would be eased to avoid ruining students distracted by what was about to unfold. Immediately, some of the "Old Blues," as we call our alumni, charged him with selling out.[8] But Brewster was determined not to have any blood on his hands. More startling, perhaps, was the immortal prophecy he shared: "In spite of my insistence on the limits of my official capacity, I personally want to say that I am appalled and ashamed that things should have come to such a pass in this country that I am skeptical of the ability of black revolutionaries to achieve a fair trial anywhere in the United States."[9] Brewster's honesty endeared him to us, but it would prove costly to his career.

Horrified by what he was hearing, U.S. Vice President Spiro Agnew opined critically, "I do not feel that students of Yale University can get a fair impression of their country under the tutelage of Kingman Brewster"— exacerbating the right-wing's paranoia that the nation's elite universities were a hotbed of liberalism and anarchy and affirmative action. More than a thousand alumni letters streamed in following Brewster's announcement, most of them supportive of his leadership, but many calling for his head.[10]

In the final days counting down to May the 1st, four thousand national guardsmen were ordered to New Haven to join local police in halting what we felt was the inevitable Armageddon, with reports swirling of stolen arms and explosives reinforcing powder-keg impressions and damaging town-gown relations at Yale. Breaking from the radicals about to run over the campus, the moderate Black Coalition in the area expressed the view that "in New Haven, as in most of the country . . . the white radical, by frantically and selfishly seeking his personal psychological release, is sharing in the total white conspiracy of denial against the black people."[11]

The final match was lit by then-National Security Advisor Henry Kissinger and President Nixon himself, when on the eve of May Day, April 30, Nixon took to the airwaves to announce an assault on Cambodia to a nation already exhausted waiting for peace to arrive in Vietnam. This only sent further shockwaves across campus, with hundreds of reporters descending on New Haven to tally the horrors about to unfold. On both offense and defense, President Brewster, working closely with his black student allies in secret meetings at his house, did his best to keep the police and protesters far apart. [12]

When May Day finally arrived, tanks were at the ready in the streets, while the Yale flagpole had been greased to avoid any violently unpatriotic displays. If they couldn't reach the flag, they couldn't burn it. Prepping the protesters that morning, Yippie leader Jerry Rubin railed, "Fuck Kingston Brewster!," and alienated the Panthers with his ridiculously immature declaration, "The most oppressed people in America are white middle-class youth. . . . We don't want to work in our daddy's business. We don't want to be a college professor, a prosecutor, or a judge. . . . We ain't never, never, never gonna grow up." [13]

The "Big Rally" kicked off at high noon, with what seemed to us like a hundred thousand protesters gathering on the Green. (The official number was around 15,000.) [14] Rock music blared. Whispers of a Weathermen presence filtered out, never to be confirmed. Mostly, though, a horde of speakers droned on into late afternoon and evening, before it was time for Beat poet Allen Ginsberg to chant his poem, which included the line, "O holy Yale Panther Pacifist Conscious populace awake alert sensitive tender." [15]

For the time being, it appeared that was going to be it. But then, at 9:30 p.m., the action shifted back to the Green, after a report, later known to be untrue, surfaced on the Yale campus that police were arresting black men upon entering. That was all it took to rile up the crowd. A half hour later, the marchers, a thousand strong, headed to the courthouse-side of the Green where they eventually collided with police teargas. A regrouping effort a few blocks away was further frustrated when a letter from "Chairman Bobby" Seale himself was read, warning the protesters not to damage the Panther cause. [16]

At that point, panic and paranoia set in, with misfired reports about Yale's gates being closed. Then, when that was about done, suddenly a pair of bombs went off in the Ingalls Rink basement, damaging the structure, but, thankfully, not taking a single human life. [17] No one knew anything for certain in the minutes and hours that followed, except that the hourglass on May Day had just about run out. I remember running through Old Campus, nose covered with a handkerchief to avoid the cloud of teargas and marijuana, as Ginsberg chanted still another mystical-political poem. So this was "the Revolution," I thought to myself.

It could have been worse, far worse. As it turned out, there were no major injuries suffered, and only twenty-one total arrests were made. [18] While the next day saw some attempts to spark another round of protests, mostly they just fizzled. Kent State was just two days away now, followed by the murder of two students at Jackson State on the 15th. The shocking violence at those two campuses would live on in national memory forever, while the events of May Day at Yale receded, except for those of us who had been there and remembered what it felt like to stand on the precipice of Armageddon, and who live to remember that noble day when the privileged students at Yale took a stand against the unlawful persecution of the members of a radical black political organization because of their revolutionary beliefs.

"Call it luck. Call it brilliant planning. Call it a conspiracy between the Man and the Panther. Whatever the reason, death and destruction passed by New Haven," Paul Bass and Doug Rae conclude in their book, *Murder in the Model City*. [19] (An excerpt appeared in the *Yale Alumni Magazine* in the July/August 2006 issue, to which I'm indebted for helping me recall the tick-tock of those intense days and months.) For many of us who witnessed this exciting time, it was the most noble moment in the history of Mother Yale.

Henry Louis Gates, Jr.
Class of '73

1   Paul Bass and Douglas W. Rae, *Murder in the Model City: The Black Panthers, Yale, and the Redemption of a Killer* (New York: Basic Books, 2006), 116.

2   Ibid., 117–119.
3   Ibid., 123.
4   Ibid., 126–127.
5   Ibid., 133 quoted.
6   Ibid., 136 quoted.
7   Ibid., 137.
8   Ibid., 138.
9   Ibid., 140.
10 Ibid., 142.

11 Ibid., 145–147.
12 Ibid., 149–152.
13 Ibid., 152–153.
14 Ibid., 153.
15 Ibid., 156.
16 Ibid., 156–158.
17 Ibid., 159.
18 Ibid., 160.
19 Ibid., p. 162.

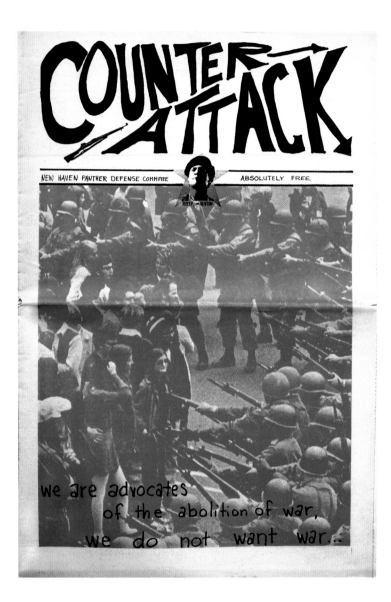

May Day at Yale, 1970: Recollections

The period from the mid-1960s until the early 1970s was one of turmoil in America and on American college and university campuses. Much has been written about this period and, to a great extent, a scholar can easily find out "what happened."

This book represents, not a "history," but the recollections of three people, a university administrator and two talented photographers, who were present at one of the most publicized events of the period. Their recollections may help people understand and visualize not only what happened, but also how it felt to be in the turmoil.

On May 1, 1970, tens of thousands of primarily young radicals from outside New Haven, Connecticut, gathered on the historic New Haven Green to protest the trial of nine Black Panther leaders.

During this period the author of this narrative was an administrator and assistant to the Yale University president, Kingman Brewster. The two photographers were residents of greater New Haven; one a faculty member in the Yale School of Art and the other a graphic designer in New Haven.

Memories put on paper more than forty years after an event can be confused and partial. Photographs can help to bring accuracy, though even photos can mislead. We have tried to be accurate and clear, and we hope the reader will get a sense of what these days were like.

The primary goal of this book is to bring together these magnificent photographs and set them in context.

The Period of Challenging Authority

Nationally, all of this was born in the post–World War II era. In that war a great many male Americans served in the armed forces; many women did as well, while other women took on men's jobs at home. By 1948 President Truman had integrated the armed forces. America was changing.

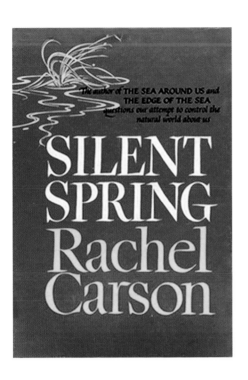

When the war was over, we had a new vision of America in which everyone, not just the old establishment, was supposed to be able to go to college, buy a car and a home, and live the American dream. Yet, as time went on, many Americans still felt, and in fact were, left out of this dream.

Many have attributed the unrest in this period to the Vietnam War. This was a profoundly unpopular war with a draft that impacted almost every male in the country. While the Vietnam War was a major factor in the unrest, it was merely one of a much larger set of issues that loomed over us, which I call the Period of Challenging Authority. A series of very significant things happened beginning with a book by Rachel Carson in 1962 called Silent Spring. This was the first popular book about the environmental damage being done to our natural eco-system – a challenge to the authority of the business/economic establishment.

The second was a book, The Feminine Mystique, by Betty Friedan published in 1963. This had a major impact on the beginning of the modern women's movement and was a challenge to the authority of a male-dominated society.

U.S. soldiers in Vietnam

The third was the assassination of President John Kennedy in 1963. Kennedy, for those of us then in our twenties, was the symbol of a new generation of young leadership. His election had been a challenge to the old political establishment.

The fourth was the assassination of Martin Luther King in April of 1968. King was, perhaps, the most significant leader of that generation, having mounted an incredibly successful, peaceful challenge to the authority of the white-dominated society.

The fifth was the assassination two months later, in June of 1968, of Robert Kennedy, President Kennedy's brother, who was running for President. Bobby Kennedy was in some ways a blend of his brother and Martin Luther King. Bobby Kennedy was a superb politician, but he was as passionate about equal rights and the plight of the poor as any white person. While King was the most significant young leader of his time, Bobby Kennedy's death, coming after King's, represented to the young of the country the final burying of our hopes for a "new America."

Finally, in 1969, there were the Stonewall Riots in Greenwich Village in which the gay and lesbian community challenged the authority of the traditional anti-gay establishment.

President John F. Kennedy speaking at Yale Commencement on June 11, 1962.

Martin Luther King, Jr. with President Kingman Brewster on June 15, 1964, the day on which he received a Yale honorary Doctor of Laws.

Atty. General Robert F. Kennedy speaking outside the Justice Department at a Congress of Racial Equality (CORE) rally, June 14, 1963

Stonewall Riots in Greewich Village, 1969.

The first outbreak of radicalism at Yale, in 1965, was not about Vietnam or any of the issues mentioned above, but rather an active student protest after a popular philosophy professor, Richard Bernstein, was not given tenure. This was a challenge by students to the old-faculty authority of the past. The author of this text was assigned by President Brewster to take charge of daily operations at Yale in response to radicalism, whether from inside or outside the University.

Radicalism and challenges to authority were everywhere nationally. One of the leading radical movements was the Black Panther Party, a group of very intelligent, politically smart young black men and women looking to better life for those not yet inheriting the "American dream." (It is important to mention women here, for it was in this period that women became leaders of major radical groups – long before they were in the "establishment.") Too little is said about how much good the Panthers did. For example, they started school breakfasts for youngsters in the inner city and worked to improve education, particularly in Oakland, their home base. Some were very radical and urged the overthrow of the American government; but most were less so and had positive goals. A major leader of the Black Panthers was Bobby Seale.

The Black Panther Murder in New Haven

In May 1969 a young member of the Black Panthers, Alex Rackley, was tortured and murdered in New Haven. It was said that he was a police informer, and three other members of the Party in New Haven were charged with his murder. But the prosecutors also indicted Bobby Seale and other Panther leaders, charging that they had orchestrated the murder. Subsequently we have learned that Rackley was not an informer and that the police and FBI could have, but did not, prevent Rackley's murder.

When it was announced in mid-March or early April of 1970 that all the defendants, including Seale, would be tried in New Haven, it became a national event. The trial was scheduled for early summer of 1970.

13

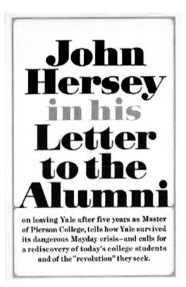

These are three excellent books which record, in detail, the events surrounding May Day at Yale. The first, *Mayday at Yale* by John Taft, was a senior essay written by a 1971 graduate. It is the best historical record of those events. It is out of print and only available in libraries. The second is *Letter to the Alumni* by the novelist John Hersey, a Yale graduate and master of one of Yale's residential colleges in 1970. The third is *Murder in the Model City* by Paul Bass and Douglas W. Rae, the former a journalist in New Haven and the latter a professor in Yale's School of Management.

Quotas May Limit College Food Plans

By CHUCK CRITCHLOW

A disagreement has arisen between the food committee and the Council of Masters over a proposal which would limit food and housing for non-Yale students this weekend.

The Council of Masters' proposal would set a quota, in accordance with city fire laws, which would permit slightly under 9000 non-Yale people to be fed and housed each day in the colleges and the Old Campus.

The quota allows for doubling the population of student-occupied rooms (with the student's permission), and limiting housing in courtyards and common rooms.

Peter Jacobi, representative from the President's office, explained the quota last night at a meeting of the Student Food Committee at Dwight Hall.

Jacobi said the problem facing the Committee is that the University will have excess food, but nowhere to feed the people.

'Be Prepared'

The university has already ordered food on the basis of crowd estimates. Yale will be prepared to feed as many as 35,000 outsiders on a given day, but acting under the quota system is only permitted to feed 9,000 within the confines of the colleges, and Old Campus.

The University Dining Hall will prepare food to be eaten on the Old Campus; College dining halls will provide meals to be eaten in college courtyards. There will be no eating inside any University dining facility.

The quota system met with instant and unanimous opposition from the students at the Dwight Hall meeting.

Objections were made on the grounds that it might provoke violence, that it was done without consulting students in the colleges, and that if adopted it would be difficult to enforce.

The final decision on the quota system has not been made.

The food committee will meet at noon today in an attempt to resolve the issue.

Regardless of whether or not the system of quotas is accepted, the University hopes to provide food in accordance with its original plans. If the system is adopted, additional space will have to be found to feed and house demonstrators.

Approximately $23,000 worth of food has been ordered for Yale students and a maximum of 76,500 meals for outsiders.

The University hopes to cover this cost with "non-coercive donations" from diners (25 cents a meal is suggested), contributions from College social fees ($5,700 has been pledged), and the regular week-end operating budget for board of $18,000.

Finger Lickin' Good

Starting Friday and continuing through Sunday, food will be served continuously from 10 in the morning to 10 at night. There will be two meals--breakfast from 10 to 4 and Dinner from 4 to 10.

The Dining Hall Department has instructed all halls to serve outside because they "couldn't possibly maintain sanitary conditions inside." The crowds would otherwise create unbearable heat, and the whole operation has to be "kept moving"--something more easily accomplished outdoors. All expressed the hope that there would be good weather.

The system will be under the direct supervision of dining hall personnel at all times.

Nevertheless, the weekend operation is heavily dependent on student volunteers. There will be 8 mealshifts and each college needs about 30 workers a shift.

So far, colleges report an inadequate turnout of volunteers.

Patient Rights Outlined

By STEPHEN LEACH

Any patient brought to Yale-New Haven Hospital this weekend will be immune from police arrest or interrogation for the duration of his treatment, except in certain situations specified by state law.

The hospital's policy in regard to the demonstrators in the event of violence was presented yesterday in a memo from Dr. Charles B. Womer, director of the hospital.

The memo states the hospital will adhere to a Connecticut statute which requires medical centers to report to the police only four types of injury.

The four injuries are gunshot wounds, knife wounds, proven rape, and dog bites.

Serve the People

"We are here to serve people who need medical care. We are not here to act as a station for the potential arrest of the people brought here," he added.

Kleinberg warned, however, "We cannot prevent the police from coming in and making an arrest if they have information about a particular patient."

The police, including Chief James F. Ahern, have reacted to the memo favorably, according to Kleinberg.

"They thought it was excellent, they were very pleased," he said.

Since cuts, abrasions, and even skull fractures are not covered by the law, the hospital will forbid even the interrogation of patients with such wounds until their release.

Kleinberg noted this could be a period of several days.

He said in many other states, "the police examine a person in a hospital, determine he has been in a riot and arrest him--you can't do this in Connecticut."

Kleinberg said the police do have the right to place under arrest a patient they bring to the hospital.

Hospital Prisoner

The patient, however, will be guarded by the hospital security staff, not by the police. No interrogation of the patient will be allowed while he is undergoing treatment.

The only other patients that will be reported to the police are extreme cases, such as a sniper who is brought to the hospital after falling from his perch and breaking his arm, said Kleinberg.

Law School Cancels Fete

The Yale Law School has cancelled its annual alumni weekend program that was scheduled for May 1-2.

The possibility of shortages of food, housing, communications, and other shortages due to the great number of people expected in New Haven for the rally this week prompted the Law School to make this decision.

John Nelson

Nearly 300 demonstrators marched from this Beinecke Plaza demonstration to various sites around the campus yesterday in an attempt to "tour Yale down."

Mass Rally Called For Ingalls Tonight

By WILLIAM BULKELEY

The Strike Steering Committee announced yesterday that the mass meeting scheduled tonight at 9 in Ingalls Rink will be devoted to a report on the plans for May Day Weekend and a discussion of the five demands.

In a release planned for circulation this morning the steering committee stated the meeting will "discuss what we have done, what we can do, what we should do now and after May Day." It will be chaired by William Farley and Kurt Schmoke, both 1971.

The first part of the meeting will be involved with the May Day plans. Douglas Miranda and several Steering Committee members will probably be among those who speak on the plans.

The rest of the meeting will be devoted to the various demands. Kenneth Mills, assistant professor of philosophy, will deliver the keynote speech and will also conclude the rally. Speakers will briefly discuss the demands. The last part of the meeting will feature open microphones to allow different people to have their views heard.

Andrew Coe, 1970, of the subcommittee for the agenda, said the meeting will probably last no more than two hours.

"Expectations" Defined

Yesterday, Georges May, Dean of Yale College, sent a letter to all chairmen of departments and directors of undergraduate studies outlining what was meant by the faculty statement that "normal expectations of the University be temporarily modified."

May said students would not be responsible for day to day work within the strike period, beginning April 27, and that postponements should be granted for term papers without penalty.

Beinecke Rally

The major event yesterday was a rally in Beinecke Plaza followed by what leaders termed "a tour of Yale," in which the demonstrators marched to various sites on campus.

Speaking to over 600 people at the demonstration, Ralph Dawson, 1971, moderator of the BSAY, said the BSAY "cannot support anything this weekend that's going to endanger the existence of the black community."

Later he added the BSAY and the community would continue to work for the demands after the weekend is over.

Dick Mann, 1970, of Yale SDS also said at the rally that the success of the strike would hinge on continuing the strike after the weekend, and "keeping the

(continued on page 3)

Law School's Teach-In Raises Legal Questions

By STEVE KANNER

A Yale Law School Teach-In which discussed the procedural and constitutional issues involved in the Panther Trial drew a full house at the Law School Auditorium last night.

Issues ranged from the political nature of the trial and questions of mass action to detailed arguments about technical legal aspects of the trial.

Ira Grudberg, a leading New Haven criminal lawyer, argued that some of the objections to the proceedings have been overblown.

He discussed the question of the legality of search without warrant pursuant to an arrest.

Restrictions on the right to this search may have been imposed by a Supreme Court ruling handed down ten days after the search of Panther Headquarters.

The question could determine whether several tapes and a gun are admitted as evidence.

Law Professor Thomas Emerson attempted to define a political trial. He argued that the present case is political if, in prosecuting the criminal offense, the state attempts to inflict injury on the Panther political movement.

While Grudberg argued that the courts "work best when not influenced by extraneous forces from the street," Emerson suggested that political activity outside the courtroom is inevitable and possibly beneficial.

In the best interests of the defendants, however, this activity should emphasize giving a fair trial, rather than supporting the Panthers' unpopular political views, Emerson noted.

"The courts are not isolated from public criticism...it is part of our freedom of expression...within certain limits" he said. "These limits are the laws of our society against non-violence."

Virtuoso pianist Van Cliburn played with the New Haven Symphony at Woolsey Hall last night. Cliburn, as always, captivated the audience with his graceful technique and sensitive interpretation.

Atmosphere Heated

Yale Girds For May 1

By SCOTT HERHOLD

Planning for the May Day rally continued on a variety of fronts yesterday, despite a growing apprehension of violent confrontation.

The major developments yesterday were:

- a statement by the BSAY declaring it would "not support anything this weekend that's going to endanger the existence of the black community;" (see accompanying story)
- a statement by the Strike Steering Committee calling for non-violence;
- the release of tentative plans for the marshalling of the rally;
- a continued study of the May Day safety precautions by a student-faculty monitoring group;
- the departure of a large number of students for the weekend;
- the reported police surveillance of the Black Panther Party headquarters on Sylvan Avenue. This was accompanied by periodic shutdowns of power at their office and Panther claims of constant police patrolling.

Non-Violence

The non-violence statement by the Strike Steering Committee came in response to demands that the National Guard be called up.

It said in part, "Our goal is to demand, to demonstrate our demands for, and to attain justice at Yale and in New Haven.... The destruction of Yale and destruction in New Haven have no place in our program."

Spokesmen for the Panther Defense Committee said a similar statement was being circulated to other colleges and universities.

Meanwhile, a monitoring group of concerned students and faculty, including Rev. William Sloane Coffin, Jr., was holding intensive discussions with the Panther Defense Committee and other groups in an effort to gauge the safety precautions for the weekend.

The group predicted it would release a statement by Thursday morning.

Marshals

Kate Fields, 1973, a coordinator of the marshals for the rally, said everything was being done to insure the non-violent nature of the demonstration.

She added that most of the marshals will be women, graduate students, or other people from New Haven, including the black community. She maintained that there were two reasons why undergraduates were not significantly involved:

- "because Yale is in some way a target of the demonstration, it would be more tactful not to have Yale undergraduates serving as marshals
- since the demonstration was called by the Panther Defense Committee, they should be in charge of marshalling it."

Miss Fields contended that women and community people would provoke a less antagonistic response from the crowd.

"The marshal can't work for peace if the crowd thinks of them as a police force," she commented.

"But if something really big happens, there's no way we can control it," she added. "All we can say is that we're working to make this non-violent."

She declined to enumerate the specific duties of the marshals, but said they would give information and other help.

Students Leaving

Meanwhile, predictions of violence provoked many Yale students to begin leaving for the weekend.

Although no one had a definite figure, Basil Henning, Master of Saybrook College, said, "I would guess that about one-third of the University is clearing out."

Their feeling was perhaps best summed up by a student who said, "I don't want my ass kicked in."

Places at Albertus Magnus College have been offered to any coeds who do not wish to remain at Yale over the weekend. In addition, many freshmen are moving from the Old Campus into residential colleges.

Police, Guida, Guard Prepare For May 1

By LEW SCHWARTZ

Recent preparations by state and local officials for the May 1 weekend have led to new plans for the New Haven Police Department and the alerting of the National Guard.

City Chief of Police James F. Ahern met with National Guard officers yesterday to consider new safety procedures.

Although the details of that meeting are not available, Adjutant-General E. Donald Walsh has called for Guard units throughout the New Haven area to be on "stand by."

According to Walsh, a New Haven unit of the National Guard will be on duty this weekend and other units in the area are on alert. But Walsh did not release the number of men involved.

The order to alert the Guard units was made Monday night.

According to Hartford press reports, Mayor Bartholomew F. Guida met informally with Connecticut Governor John N. Dempsey earlier in the week to ask him for national Guard aid if needed this weekend.

The move was termed a "precautionary measure" by state officials.

Guida Statement

These preparations follow a statement by Guida released last week.

"Peaceful protest, peaceful dissent, and peaceful assembly are all part of the American heritage," the mayor said.

"My responsibility is to maintain to the extent humanly possible a climate in this community that is free of repression and violence, for the sake of the citizens of our community, for the sake of those who come to our community to peacefully protest, and for the sake of those who are on trial," he added.

Police Busy

The New Haven police have reportedly activated a series of plans for the weekend. Working shifts will most likely be increased from eight to twelve hours daily beginning tonight.

Some unofficial reports say the police will patrol in 16-hour shifts by Friday, and the police auxiliary will aid the main force.

One source commented on an increase in "new faces", presumably signifying an influx of extra help from state and federal sources.

The police preparations follow three recent robberies involving the theft of 500 guns in the area during the last two weeks.

A truck loaded with shot guns and rifles and hijacked last Sunday night was recovered Monday in Bronx, N.Y. None of the weapons were found.

In that robbery, 280 riot guns and 80 .22 caliber rifles were stolen.

Earlier, a sporting goods store in Newington and a truck in Fairfield were robbed.

Plaza Pickets

Yalies Protest In New York

By JEFFREY MAYER

J. Richardson Dilworth, a member of the Yale Corporation and the Chairman of Rockefeller Center, said yesterday that "there is still a question as to whether it is appropriate for the Yale Corporation to take action" on the Strike demands.

He cautioned, however, that he was in no position to comment personally on the situation at Yale or to speak for the Yale Corporation.

Speaking in his 56th floor office overlooking Rockefeller Center in downtown Manhattan, Dilworth expressed anxiety over the approaching May Day weekend. He said he was hopeful there would be no violence, but feared "a minor or major bloodbath."

Armed Citizens?

Dilworth said he had received reports of New Haven residents arming themselves, but said he has not been at Yale recently to be able to comment further.

Dilworth did say he has received numerous phone calls demanding Brewster's ouster.

The Rockefeller Center chairman expressed these and other points at a meeting with three Yale seniors, Geoff Davis, Barry Brankin, and David Weinberg, who discussed the strike and presented and explained the student demands.

"He's now in a position where he can't ignore us," Brankin commented after the meeting.

The interview came as 25 Yale students picketed 56 floors below at the corner of 50th Street and Rockefeller Plaza.

The students carried signs reading "Stop Repression," "Free All Political Prisoners," and a meticulously designed silkscreen depicting the scales of justice balancing overweight "moral paralysis" against the lighter "justice beyond the courts."

As David Schweizer, spokesman for the group explained to the transient noon-time crowds, the group was urging people to be "concerned for the suppression of the Black Panthers since their problem is everybody's problem."

"We call upon the Yale Corporation," he continued, "to support us in our plea for a fair trial for the Panthers and responsibility in Yale's relationship with New Haven."

Group To Continue

According to Schweizer, the group intends to follow up yesterday's demonstration with other actions.

"We don't see May 1 as an ending point," he said. "We hope this group will continue to act in the future."

(continued on page 3)

Jeff Mayer

25 Yale students walked New York's sidewalks yesterday to picket the offices of Yale Corporation member J. Richardson Dilworth. Carrying signs reading "Stop Repression" and "Free All Political Prisoners," the students evoked noticeable reactions from one incredulous Yale alumnus, police, and several passersby.

Agnew Attacks Brewster

Asks End To King's Reign

By RICHARD FUCHS

Vice President Spiro Agnew called last night for the removal of Kingman Brewster Jr. as president of Yale.

Speaking before a Republican fund-raising dinner in Hollywood Beach, Florida, Agnew said, "It is time for the alumni of that prestigious university to demand it be headed by a more mature and responsible person than Kingman Brewster."

Earlier in the evening, over 1500 Yale undergraduates signed a petition supporting Brewster.

Agnew's comments culminated five days of widespread criticism of Brewster in the national media, dating back to the release Thursday night of the Yale president's statement on the Black Panther trial in New Haven.

At that time, Brewster had said he was "skeptical of the ability of black revolutionaries to receive a fair trial anywhere in the United States."

Immaturity

Agnew characterized that statement as "unnecessary and immature."

"I do not feel that students at Yale University can get a proper education under the leadership of Kingman Brewster," the vice president said.

Agnew's remarks on Brewster were delivered in a speech in which he called on the nation's universities to treat student mobs as though they were wearing "brown shirts or white sheets."

He said campus peace through appeasement "is not worth the price. That sell-out is intellectual treason; better confrontation than a cave-in."

He called for immediate expulsion for students who violate college rules, no negotiations with demonstrating students while "coercion" exists, and no amnesty for violence or lawlessness.

Sevareid

Agnew has not been alone in his criticism of Brewster. CBS radio and television commentator Eric Sevareid lashed out at him on nationwide TV last night.

He said, "There are some ominous signs that this coming May Day weekend will be Yale's turn. Yale has been relatively quiescent. A fair portion of its student body now feels the springtime urge to prove their

(continued on page 3)

Graduate Students Give Strike Limited Support

By SAM SWARTZ

Although most of Yale's response to the New Haven 9 trial has come from undergraduates, graduate and professional students have not been entirely inactive.

The Schools of Drama, Art, Divinity, and Music have voted to allow suspension of classes.

Although the Medicine and Law Schools have rejected institutional shutdowns, students in both are applying professional skills to the May Day and New Haven 9 movements.

The Art and Architecture School approved Friday, by a vote of 84-16, a resolution to strike and redirect their efforts.

Students and faculty voted Monday to open some areas of the Art and Architecture Building to 500 May Day weekend visitors, 200 to sleep on rugs and 300 on floors.

Since the meeting Friday, the students have formed several separate action groups.

Stop Repression Now

One of the groups is producing "Free the Panther 9" and "Stop Repression Now" posters, which will be put up around New Haven later this week.

According to art student Larry Rosen, the posters are not "aesthetic room decorations," but are produced to "serve towards the educative power of the people."

The May 1st Media Group, also from the Art and Architecture School, plans to "document the events in New Haven related to the Panther trial" in 16mm film, still photography, sound, and videotape, according to their posters.

After the documentation has been assembled, it will be available to anyone who wishes to see it.

The Art and Architecture faculty voted Thursday to conduct an exhibition of donated work for sale.

Proceeds will go into a fund to "deal with any financial aspects that might arise from the present situation," according to a faculty spokesman.

(continued on page 3)

Arrests For Bomb Charge

New Haven Police Chief James F. Ahern announced today the arrest of two suspects on charges of possession of explosives with intent to cause injury.

The two, James Herms, an ex-Yale freshman and a former Weatherman, and Greg Wells, an evening student at Southern Connecticut State College, were arrested at their home in a cooperative residence at 361 Elm Street.

Ahern indicated that the explosives were intended to be used in the upcoming weekend demonstration in support of the Panthers.

Police, who obtained a search warrant previous to the arrest, said they found a quantity of smoke grenades and "chemical compounds prepared for explosives" in the suspects' third floor room.

Police have confiscated all the items which, according to one cooperative member, included several containers and glass jars

(continued on page 3)

Yale Daily News

National Guard troops in front of the Yale Daily News building
Thursday afternoon, the day before May Day.

Tom Strong

In the legal events leading up to the trial, one day in court two Panther members were in the back of the courtroom quietly reading newspapers, while the white people were chatting aloud and reading. The judge slammed down his gavel and summarily sentenced the two black men to jail for contempt of court. This event, along with the trial itself, brought national reaction.

Even Yale's president spoke out, saying at a faculty meeting: "In spite of my insistence on the limits of my official capacity, I personally want to say that I am appalled and ashamed that things should have come to such a pass in this country that I am skeptical of the ability of black revolutionaries to achieve a fair trial anywhere in the United States." Everyone from the Vice President of the United States to many Yale alumni called for Brewster's removal. Radicals, not just the Panthers but radicals of every sort, decided that they would all descend on New Haven for a rally on May 1, 1970. The radical rhetoric called for Yale to be burned down and the city destroyed. It soon became clear that we had to expect tens of thousands of radicals coming to New Haven and to Yale. And so, under Brewster's leadership, we were tasked with figuring out what to do to keep Yale safe.

The Political Environment

On the right was Richard Nixon, who we subsequently learned had advocated for an explosion on an elite campus, hoping this would move the middle class into his political camp.

J. Edgar Hoover was head of the FBI and a conservative. He had almost unlimited power, and we subsequently learned he was being informed daily about events at Yale and that the FBI was tapping phones. The mayor of New Haven, Bartholomew Guida, did not like Yale. He saw Yale, in part correctly, as the mansion on the hill, arrogant and "above it all." Yale, at that time, had no community relations program. Guida called in his police chief, James Ahern, and told him (as Ahern reported to the author), "If there is any rioting or danger, you are to funnel it all onto the Yale campus, and save the city." Happily, Ahern was a close personal friend and we were able to construct some alternative plans without the mayor's knowledge.

Ericka Huggins   *Kathleen Cleaver*

Two of the major Black Panther women leaders.

"... a group of students had decided to publish a free daily report of campus events in coordination with the Student Strike Commitee. (Yale's radio station, WYBC, supported the strike, but the Yale Daily News *was editorially opposed to it and remained so until after May Day.) The stated purpose of the* Strike Newspaper *was to 'provide a flow of information within the Yale community and from the Yale community to the outside media.' The group established itself in Dwight Hall, where a printing press was available and where the newspaper's staff was welcomed. The* Strike Newspaper *began publishing on Thursday [April 23] and issued a great deal of information in a way that encouraged the strike. Its very existence tended to give the strike a coloring of legitimacy, especially after the paper received positive support from the Council of Masters [of Yale's residential colleges]. Before long, other prostrike organizations were also assisted by the administration."*

From Mayday at Yale *(pages 74-75) by John Taft*

wtnh, Chanel 8

hairspiration.blogspot.com 30 July 2011

16

STRIKE NEWSPAPER

YALE UNIVERSITY   MAY 1 1970   436-1480; 436-1481; 432-0302

This newspaper is FREE — share it!

MAY DAY

Below is a summary of latest reports on arrangements for the MayDay weekend along with some summaries of recommended procedure. A steering Committee meeting last night set these plans as final. Committee members will be staffing information phones, 436-0115 throughout the weekend. Any changes of plan can be checked there.

SCHEDULE

Friday, at 10:30 a.m., a press conference in front of the Courthouse, with representatives of the Black Panther Party, the Panther Defense Committee and the Chicago Seven. From 12 to 4, rock music on the Green. From 4 to 7, the rally. Abbie Hoffman, Dave Dellinger, Carol Brightman, Big Man. Saturday, from 10 to 12 noon, workshops in Yale buildings: Linsley Chit, Woolsey Hall, Strathcona, and Connecticut Hall. More from 12 to 4. At 4, a rally on the Green: Artie Seale, Tom Hayden, John Froines, Jean Ganet, Ralph Abernathy, and others. Sunday, Black Music Festival. The location will be announced.

INFORMATION CENTERS

May Day information will be available at five constantly staffed centers: Panther Defense Committee headquarters, 1084 Chapel Street; Connecticut Hall, Room 78; The Exit, Elm and College Streets; and Bread and Roses, 538 State Street. Call 60115, or see the phone numbers list.

FIRST AID

Gas: it feels like hell, but it won't really hurt you. Wash. Rinse your eyes, wash your skin. Change clothes if you can. Cover your mouth and nose with a wet mask; cover your eyes with goggles or glasses. Don't wear lenses. Don't try vaseline unless you can wipe it off immediately. And don't panic.

Fainting: Head down, legs up. Talk. Bleeding: Firm pressure with a clean cloth. Get to an aid station. Blood looks scary, but you can spare a lot.

(Cont. on back page)

TRIAL HISTORY

On May 21, 1969 the body of Alex Rackley was found in a swamp in Middlefield, Conn. The next day Warren Kimbro, Ericka Huggins, Margaret Hudgins, Rose Marie Smith, Jeannie Wilson, Maude Francis, Frances Carter and George Edwards were arrested in New Haven. All were charged with murder and conspiracy to commit murder. Police sources stated an informant had seen the deceased at 365 Orchard St. "and had witnessed an effort to compel him to confess to being a suspected infiltrator and informant for law enforcement agencies." On May 28 Loretta Luckes was arrested on the same charges and on June 6 Lonnie McLucas was arrested in Salt Lake City, Utah, and Landon Williams and Rory Hithes were arrested in Denver, Colo.

On June 23 the New Haven Superior
(Cont. on page three)

BALTIMORE

According to an Associated Press release yesterday, Baltimore police have arrested 18 persons described by police as Black Panthers, sympathizers, and associates. All were arrested on charges stemming from the death of Eugene L. Anderson, whose body was found last July. Four of those arrested — were charged with homicide, 4 with "other crimes," and 6 were wanted as state witnesses, said the A.P.

The New Haven Panther Defense Committee yesterday reiterated its hope for a peaceful weekend, despite events in Baltimore and the presence of troops in New Haven. A spokesman said of the arrests, "If this doesn't show people what's happening in this country, I don't know what does." Of the rally she said, "We really don't think there's anything to worry about if people realize what we're doing and why."

COMMENT

The arrests in Baltimore yesterday could not have been better timed to inflame an already tense situation. This action undermines the efforts of everyone here for peaceful, non-violent demonstration. It is to the government's advantage for New Haven to erupt into violence. Every time there is a riot, Richard Nixon and Spiro Agnew gain popularity in the United States. Too much is at stake to risk a violent confrontation. A riot in New Haven would not only turn America against the Panthers, but also against Yale, students, and all who have worked so diligently to end injustice in this country.

There are thousands of well-armed troops dispersed in and around New Haven; they are there for one reason — the struggle must go on, but on our terms, not on theirs; a debacle would in no way help Bobby Seale and the Panthers.

Newspapers throughout the United States have played down the New Haven demonstration thus far, and few people outside of the East know very much about it. If there is a riot, everyone will know about it, but all they will know is that New Haven was wrecked by "a bunch of hippies, radicals, and effete intellectuals." This will not help our cause. We must stand together and double our efforts for a NON-VIOLENT demonstration. It is the only way.

Dale Kutnick
DALE KUTNICK

panther conference

David Hilliard, Chief of Staff of the Black Panther Party; Big Man, Editor of the Panther newspaper, and Sister Carol Smith spoke at a press conference at New Haven Panther Headquarters yesterday morning.

Sister Carol read a press statement which said, in part, "not only do we need Black support but we need support from all the poor and oppressed people And the alienated children of the ruling class."

The statement went on to emphasize the present need for action. "This does not mean arbitrary confrontation, rampages through the streets and knocking old women -- we can't be anarchistic and emotional, we have to be clear-headed and organized." The statement cited the efforts of student canvassers in the white community. "An example of this type of clear-headedness is the fact that Yale students cut their hair and took the time to go into White middle-class communities to rally support for this trial and for the cause of justice in the United States."

The Party's role among other groups working toward this weekend's demonstration of concern for justice in the trial was also clarified. "It is not the Party's place to tell supporters what to do or what to say but our duty is to tell all of you about what is necessary for survival in Amerikka."

The Party also shunned the initiation of any violence. "The people and the Party won't cause violence in the courts, the schools or the streets..."

Hilliard and Big Man then answered questions. Big Man stressed the Party's repudiation of recent media reports that the Panthers intend to incite violence,

A rumor of a bust at Panther headquarters last night drew 100 students to Branford courtyard and several to Panther HQ. They learned that police had been present but left again; no arrests took place.

(Cont. on back page)

TROOPS

In response to a request from New Haven Mayor Bart Guida, Gov. Dempsey has called out the National Guard. Under the command of Brigadier General Edward Wozenski, of Bristol, task force Bravo is already deployed throughout the greater New Haven area. Estimated at around 3,000 men, the Guard is presently stationed at Goff St. armory, among other locations.

Also joining the fun are 4,000 federal troops, stationed on the ready at Westover Air Force Base, in Massachusetts, and Quonset Naval Base, in Rhode Island, paratroopers and marines. According to press sources, the feds are four hours from New Haven.

So the dangers to Yale were not just from the radical left, but also from the Nixon-Mitchell right and even the mayor of New Haven.

Preparation

As May Day approached, the nation became more nervous about what might happen. The attorney general sent an assistant attorney general to camp out here and keep an eye on things. The FBI sent extra agents into town. The CIA sent people here, as they believed foreign radicals would join in.

About 4,000 national guardsmen were mobilized and a plan for their deployment was developed. Marines were sent to the Naval base in Newport, R.I., with helicopters to bring them to town if needed. More than 200 state troopers prepared to move in, and every New Haven and Yale police officer was told they would have to be on duty for at least thirty-six hours.

Two men were ultimately most responsible for "keeping the peace" on this tumultuous weekend. One was Yale's president, Kingman Brewster. The other was the relatively young New Haven police chief, James Ahern. Ahern was one of the few police officers in the country at that time who had studied modern methods for controlling large crowds and preventing rioting.

Perhaps the most significant event was that we were able to convince the state police, the National Guard, and the Marines to allow Chief Ahern to be in command of all the forces. It was the only time in American history, before or after, when a local police chief was put in such control.

We have all thought about the great philosophical question of whether the ends justify the means. This was the first time for many of us when we knew that "lives were on the line." In attempting to keep the peace, we did things that were not always ethical. But we did them believing that preventing deaths and major destruction were what was important.

Chaplain William Sloane Coffin.

The University decided to react to all this in a very different way than had other universities facing similar difficulties. We concluded that there was no way we could keep everyone out of the campus and, while doing so, prevent serious injury or death and damage to Yale property.

We had six weeks available to develop a strategy.

Because President Brewster and I knew that our phones were tapped (but not who was doing it) and that the radicals had convinced staff at Yale to pass internal documents to them, we decided to make very little of our strategy available to everyone, particularly in writing. Rather, we decided to roll out our plans, making some moves public only at the last minute. Brewster was a pragmatic man eager to not be restricted and be able to "duck and weave" as necessary. We consulted with deans, faculty, students, masters of residential colleges, Chief Ahern, and community radical leaders, and we would learn new and valuable ideas from everyone. Throughout the planning period and the weekend itself, Yale's great chaplain, William Sloane Coffin, was an independent force for good.

We decided that the ends – particularly preventing death and injury – did justify means that might not always be admired. We believed we should not stand on principle alone, but that we should be quick to change our minds if someone had a better solution to a given problem. In short, we did something that is so feared today – we made compromises.

As the schedule promised, there were rallies on the Green on Friday and Saturday. Dan Bellucci, New Haven music buff, confirms that at least two of the promised fifteen musical groups performed: McCoy Tyner and The UP.

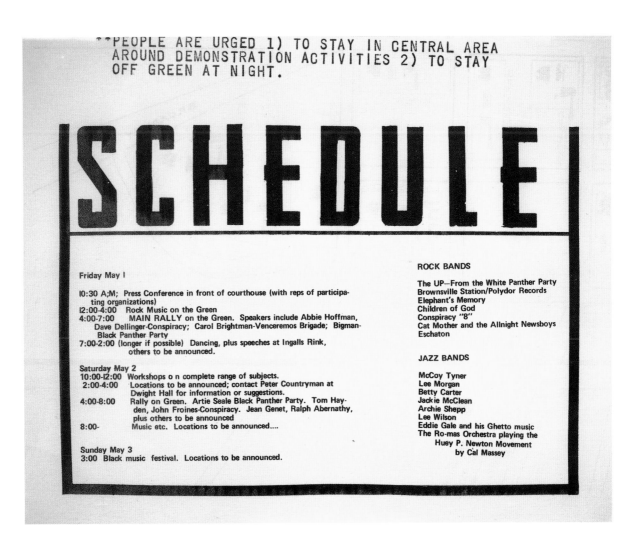

Our "strategy" had three parts

First, we wanted to prevent death and human injury, and the destruction of Yale property.

Second, we did not want to disrupt the ongoing academic process.

Third, we had learned that virtually all the radical students at Yale, most of the radicals in New Haven, and many of the national radicals were people who had serious goals for social change and were not "dangerous" people – and I include most of the Panthers in that group. But there were a relatively small number of radicals – such as the so-called Weathermen – who did not hesitate to kill and to destroy property. We did not want to "push" the moderate radicals together with the dangerous radicals.

This was a time of rhetoric. The Internet did not exist; most comment about social change came in the form of the spoken word. It was loud; the language was often obscene and it went on and on. Yet for the moderate radicals, whatever they may have said did not always reflect all of their feelings.

The moderate radicals had high ideals, and they were pushing those ideals to the edge of accepted behavior. If one does this in life, it is often helpful to have an anchor in case things go wrong – perhaps a parent or a good friend. We had learned that it was critical not to worry about the harsh rhetoric and even difficult behavior, because we wanted those radicals to see us as people always willing to listen.

NOW THE SILENCE IS ENDED... In the spring of 1970, on campuses across the nation, the acrid odor of tear gas replaced the fragrance of freshly blooming flowers. And choruses of "power to the people" echoed through dormitories and classrooms. Since that time there has been silence. Now the silence is ended with **PETER ROSEN'S** penetrating documentary of Yale Universities time of turmoil and the reactions of her Alumni in **'BRIGHT COLLEGE YEARS'**

IN COLOR
AN AVCO EMBASSY R

Courtesy of Avco Embassy Picture Corp.

Bright College Years, 1971, *a 52-minute-long documentary of the Yale protests against Nixon's bombing of Cambodia (1970) was filmed and directed by Peter Rosen who made the film while studying at Yale's film-making program. . . . He is able to illustrate what is happening quite clearly without having to use a voiceover narration, and he allows people of all persuasions to speak for themselves. This includes alumni arriving to attend a homecoming football game, student protest leaders and radical activist Abbie Hoffman. Another issue the filmmakers explore is student reaction to the arrest of Bobby Seale and other Black Panther leaders in New Haven.*

From a review by Clarke Fountain, *Rovi*

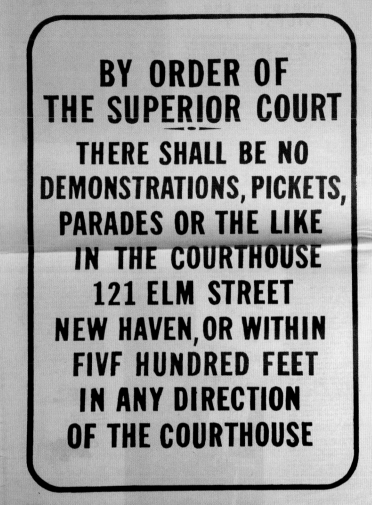

We believed that many of the national radicals were also moderate, despite their rhetoric.

We invited all the radicals who came to town to stay in the courtyards of the residential colleges, and we fed them for two days – lettuce, rice, granola, and water. Each college had a role: one was a place for younger children to be safe; another was for the radical motorcycle groups; another was a first aid station.

Every Yale student was allowed to go home and very few did so, but rather stayed and helped.

Having set ourselves a strategy, we had to focus on the tactics we would use to achieve it.

From the early 1960s when Yale began to admit ever larger numbers of minorities, the University devoted a great deal of time to work with the minority student groups – at that time primarily the black students and the then-called "Chicano" students, now referred to as Hispanic.

the power of the pigs

Recently, a shoot-out took place on Congress Avenue in New Haven whereby two black men exchanged gunfire; one was killed and the other turned himself in to the police.

Witnesses on the scene provided the following account of what happened:

Fred Smith had gone into a small store on Congress Avenue operated by a bookie named Hawley--also known as a dealer in stolen goods and drugs, especially heroin. Fred's mood was jubilant when he entered the store because he had just hit the numbers for $2000. and had come to collect. Hawley did not share Fred's good spirits at the prospect of losing $2000 and apparently decided against suffering such a loss. He blatantly refused to pay off and, in order to curb the ensuing argument, ran Fred out of the store with a gun. He fired at Fred outside the store and two of the shots tore through his clothing. Someone tossed Fred a .32 which he immediately used to defend himself; fortunately, for his own safety, he didn't miss.

Although this was a clear-cut case of self-defense, the story that was broadcast over the news media blew everyone in the neighborhoods's mind--for they heard that their buddy hadn't just shot a bookie (in self-defense), but had "murdered" a police agent, a nigger pig whose bookie joint was actually a pig station set up by Chief Pig Ahern to perpetrate dope and crime in the Congo while keeping himself informed of all "offenders' so as to be able to make periodic "clean-ups". In fact, such a "clean up" commenced immediately after the incident.

The pigs called Hawley a "hero who was killed in the line of duty,' had the City declare a day of mourning in his honor, held Fred on charges of first degree murder with no bail, and proceeded to raid the entire area arresting some 25-30 people on the first night. The raids continued for several days terrorizing the entire neighborhood.

Once again, the pigs were oinking in the faces of black people and the people dug their own powerlessness against the oppressor--just as they had in '67 when the pigs had occupied their community with hundreds of State Troopers armed to the teeth with high-powered weapons.

The Hawley case raised a lot of questions in the minds of New Haveners. For example, the use of the people's tax dollars to set up an illegal operation was questioned by even conservative whites. Blacks were asking what happens to all the money earned from so highly profitable a racket--run by the pigs? Whey were just addicts and small-time hustlers getting busted instead of the bankers and pushers? Surely Hawley had established connections with his counterparts in other areas. Were these people paying off, and if so, who was getting the bread? Was it Ahern alone who was profiting from these criminal transactions? How many other pig operations existed in the black community, and how many other undercover agents were around? questions may never be learned, but black people must realize that the pigs will continue to flood our communities with dope and set up their crime traps as long as they can get away with it.

We, black people, have no power with which to prevent Redevelopment from tearing down our neighborhoods and replacing them with highways and parking facilities for suburbanites. We have no power to prevent the city from raising taxes and rents for public housing. We have no power to elect people who will represent our interests. We have no power to deal with slumlords who subject us to inhuman living conditions and our children to lead paint poisoning. We have no power to improve the quality of education and medical care for our people. We've experienced this powerlessness over and over again as we've watched our every effort for hundreds of years to develop and apply political power go down the proverbial drain. We must therefore understand that our political power will grow only out of the barrel of a gun. That just as the Vietnamese could not "talk" the U.S. Imperialists out of their country, we cannot "talk" the pigs out of our communities. That we must begin to deliver political consequences to the pigs each and every time they oink in our faces as in the Hawley case. Blacks should not have allowed 25-30 brothers to be dragged from their homes and off the block by the pigs. We must let the pigs know that when they come into our community, it's at their own risk.

It's time we stopped repressing our anger until it explodes at each other. We've got to understand that our black brother or sister is not our enemy. Our enemy is the racist capitalist system which exploits and robs us of human needs, rights, and dignity. The first line of offense and defense of this pig power structure is the police force which now occupies the black community like the gestapo--controlling, repressing, watchdogging, and brutalizing our people, and perpetuating our crime. As long as people refuse to see who the real enemy is and refuse to understand that war has been declared on black people just as it was on the Vietnamese (unofficially and illegally), we will remain in our present condition of slavery subjected to the wanton violence of the pigs at any given time.

Seize the Time to Use Our Power

FREE BOBBY NEW HAVEN MAY 1

10

PRISON, where is thy victory ?

When a person studies mathematics, he learns that there are many mathematical laws which determine the approach he must take to solving the problems presented to him. In the study of geometry, one of the first laws a person learns is that "the whole is not greater than the sum of its parts." This means simply that one cannot have a geometrical figure such as a circle or a square which in its totality, contains more than it does when broken down into smaller parts. Therefore, if all the smaller parts add up to a certain amount, the entire figure cannot add up to a larger amount. The prison cannot have a victory over the prisoner, because those in charge take the same kind of approach and assume if they have the w whole body in a cell that they have there all that makes up the person. But a prisoner is not a geometrical figure, and an approach which is successful in mathematics, is wholly unsuccessful when dealing with human beings.

In the case of the human, we are not dealing only with the single individual, we are also dealing with the ideas and beliefs which have motivated him and which sustain him, even when his body is confined. In the case of humanity, the whole is much greater than its parts, because the whole includes the body which is measurable and confinable, and also the ideas which cannot be measured and which cannot be confined. The ideas are not only within the mind of the prisoner where they cannot be seen nor controlled, the ideas are also within the people. The ideas which can and will sustain our movement for total freedom and dignity of the people, cannot be imprisoned, for they are to be found in the people, all the people, wherever they are. As long as the people live by the ideas of freedom and dignity there will be no prison which can hold our movement down. Ideas move from one person to another in the association of brothers and sisters who recognize that a most evil system of capitalism has set us against each other, when our real enemy is the exploiter who profits from our poverty. When we realize such an idea then we come to love and appreciate our brothers and sisters who we may have seen as enemies, and those exploiters who we may have seen as friends are revealed for what they truly are to all oppressed people. The people are the idea, the respect and dignity of the people, as they move toward their freedom is the sustaining force which reaches into and out of the prison. The walls, the bars, the guns and the guards can never encircle or hold down the idea of the people. And the people must always carry forward the idea which is their dignity and their beauty.

The prison operates with the idea that when it has a person's body it has his entire being--since the whole cannot be greater than the sum of its parts. They put the body in a cell, and seem to get some sense of relief and security from that fact. The idea of prison victory then, is that when the person in jail begins to act, think, and believe the way they want him to, then they have won the battle and the person is then "rehabilitated." But this cannot be the case, because those who operate the prisons, have failed to examine their own beliefs thoroughly, and they fail to understand the types of people they attempt to control. Therefore, even when the prison thinks it has won the victory, there is no victory.

There are two types of prisoners. The largest number are those who accept the legitimacy of the assumptions upon which the society is based. They wish to acquire the same goals as everybody else, money, power, greed and conspicuous consumption. In order to do so, however, they adopt techniques and methods which the society has defined as illegitimate. When this is discovered such people are put in jail. They may be called "illegitimate capitalists" since their aim is to acquire everything this capitalistic society defines as legitimate. The second type of prisoner, is the one who rejects the legitimacy of the assumptions upon which the society is based. He argues that the people at the bottom of the society are exploited for the profit and advantage of those at the top. Thus, the oppressed exist, and will always be used to maintain the privileged status of the exploiters. There is no sacredness, there is no dignity in either exploiting or being exploited. Although this system may make the society function at a high level of technological efficiency, it is an illegitimate system, since it rests upon the suffering of humans who are as worthy and as dignified as those who do not suffer. Thus, the second type of prisoner says that the society is corrupt and illegitimate and must be overthrown. This second type of prisoner is the political prisoner. They do not accept the legitimacy of the society and cannot participate in its corrupting exploitation. whether they are in the prison or on the block.

The prison cannot gain a victory over either type of prisoner no matter how hard it tries. The "illegitimate capitalist" recognizes that if he plays the game the prison wants him to play, he will have his time reduced and be released to continue his activities. Therefore, he is willing to go through the prison programs and do the things he is told. He is willing to say the things the prison authorities want to hear. The prison assumes he is "rehabilitated" and ready for the society. The prisoner has really played the prison's game so that he can be released to resume pursuit of his capitalistic goals. There is no victory, for the prisoner from the git-go accepted the idea of the society He pretends to accept the idea of the prison as a part of the game he has always played.

The prison cannot gain a victory over the political prisoner because he has nothing to be rehabilitated from or to. He refuses to accept the legitimacy of the system and refuses to participate. To participate is to admit that the society is legitimate because of its exploitation of the oppressed. This is the idea which the political prisoner does not accept, this is the idea for which he has been imprisoned, and this is the reason why he cannot cooperate with the system. The political prisoner will, in fact, serve his time just as will the "illegitimate capitalist." Yet the idea which motivated the political prisoner reststs in the people, and all the prison has is a body.

The dignity and beauty of man rests in the human spirit which makes him more than simply a physical being. This spirit must never be suppressed for exploitation by others. As long a as the people recognize the beauty of their human spirits and move against suppression and exploitation, they wi will be carrying out one of the most beautiful ideas of all time. Because the human whole is much greater than the sum of its parts, the ideas will always be among the people. The prison cannot be victorious because walls, bars and guards cannot conquer or hold down an idea.

ALL POWER TO THE PEOPLE!

BLACK POWER TO
BLACK PEOPLE
AND PANTHER POWER TO
THE VANGUARD.

Huey P. Newton
Minister of Defense
Black Panther Party

PRISON, WHERE IS THY VICTORY

YOU CAN'T
JAIL A
REVOLUTION

11

Yale Strike News publication from May Day: front and back covers, page 21.

Deans, masters of colleges, and senior administrators worked to develop relationships, to encourage and assist in every aspect of the students' lives and, particularly, to develop first-class academic programs related to minority groups. Provost Charles Taylor spent an enormous amount of his time with a committee of the Black Student Alliance at Yale (BSAY) to bring about the Black Studies major. By doing these things, we all had developed personal relationships with the minority students and their leadership. This investment of our and the students' time paid dividends during May Day weekend.

Above: Huey P. Newton, co-founder and Commander of All Revelutionary Forces, Black Panthers.

"A proposal to the movement by Youth Against War & Fascism," poster published at 58 West 25th Street, New York, May 1, 1970.

What is needed in New Haven:

A call for a People's Assembly to free the Panthers — NOW!

The pigs murdered Fred Hampton in his bed; they murdered Mark Clark and little Bobby Hutton; Huey is in prison and Eldridge was hounded out of the country by racist dogs. The time to stop them is NOW!

They've taken the New York Panther 21, the New Haven 9, the sisters and brothers in Chicago, Los Angeles, Jersey City and everywhere that the Black Panther Party has raised the standard of Black liberation and thrown them into concentration camps in true Hitlerite fashion.

Now they want to go all the way and execute the Chairman of the Black Panther Party as a symbol of terror against the whole Black liberation struggle from coast to coast. Millions of people have awakened with indignation, outrage and hatred for the Nazi-like atrocities and have come to realize that the hour of decision in New Haven is approaching. The time to free the Panthers is NOW!

The war of extermination against the heroic Black Panther Party by the Nixon-Agnew-Mitchell Administration is of national and international significance. It is of the gravest concern to the 25 million Black people and to the people everywhere who oppose racism and support the Black liberation struggle.

Bobby Seale might have been kidnapped in any town in the U.S.; Panthers have been framed up all across the country; the hour of decision in the struggle for the existence of the Panther Party is coming in New Haven. There can be no valid local restricion upon the struggle; it is the duty of everyone everywhere to do their utmost to see that the Panthers in New Haven are freed.

Mere ceremonial demonstrations, even large ones, have their time and place. However, the burning need of the hour is to establish in New Haven a popular organ of the people which will do what is needed NOW! This PEOPLE'S ASSEMBLY will in fact represent the millions across the country who really want to see the infamous, racist frameup ended. The PEOPLE'S ASSEMBLY should be so constituted as to have the broad confidence of the masses so that it can effectively counteract the conspiratorial clique of racist, imperialist usurpers who masquerade as the representatives of the people in New Haven but who are persecuting, in a fascist manner, true representatives of the people, such as the Black Panthers.

What is needed in order to insure that we do not witness another protest followed by an execution—as in the cases of Sacco-Vanzetti, the Rosenbergs, et al.—is for the movement to immediately establish in New Haven a center which would become a magnet to draw thousands upon thousands of people from all over the country. By their overwhelming presence they could exert great power and influence in New Haven to see that this outrageous frameup is ended—NOW!

A broad coalition of groups firmly united on one common objective—on the willingness, determination and ability to see that the legal lynching of the Panthers is stopped now — should convoke a PEOPLE'S ASSEMBLY. This would let the New Haven pig structure know that the people aren't going to permit a frameup. The ASSEMBLY would summon the people together to deliberate upon measures to achieve the objective for which it was constituted—freeing the Panthers NOW—and it should function continuously until its objective is achieved.

The PEOPLE'S ASSEMBLY will in fact have derived its authority from the popular will of the millions of people throughout the country and the world who share its convictions. The ASSEMBLY will be in sharp contrast to the reactionary clique of New Haven conspirators, the cops, courts and politicians who do the dirty work for the exploiters.

The PEOPLE'S ASSEMBLY will have the confidence of the millions because it will function publicly and democratically in order to carry out the will of the people who don't want to leave the Panthers to the tender mercies of the Ku Klux Klan in black robes and pig uniforms. Again, this will be in contrast to the racist authorities who are widely discredited among the people. It is they who have connived and conspired with the Nixon-Agnew-Mitchell forces behind the backs of the people to carry out the racist frameup of the Panthers. They secretly plotted to tear to shreds the democratic rights of the people.

The PEOPLE'S ASSEMBLY will take vigorous measures to countermand and undo the illegal, unconstitutional assaults upon the Black Panther Party. By their direct participation, all who attend the ASSEMBLY will in fact be delegates for the millions who want the Panthers free. It will be a legitimate authority precisely because it seeks to reverse the illegitimate measures by which the police and the courts conspired to illegally transport (kidnap) Bobby Seale from San Francisco without a warrant; to illegally extradite him into the waiting arms of the New Haven racists who were known in advance to be bent upon the destruction of the Panthers; to indict the New Haven Panthers through an illegally constituted grand jury that was handpicked by the local sheriff from his own pack of cronies.

Participation in the PEOPLE'S ASSEMBLY should be based upon one criterion and only one — the genuine will to devote all energies and resources to see to it that this frameup is ended NOW!

Let us call the people together in New Haven and stay there, STAY THERE, STAY THERE for as long as it takes and do whatever is necessary to free the Panthers. No more genocide, no more lynchings, no more frameups, no more Panthers in jail!

BUILD THE PEOPLE'S ASSEMBLY!
BUILD THE PEOPLE'S POWER!
SEIZE THE TIME NOW!

SEIZE THE TIME

A proposal to the movement by Youth Against War & Fascism

58 West 25th St.
New York, N.Y. 10010

Tel: 242-9225, 675-2520

May 1, 1970

Kurt Schmoke, later the mayor of Baltimore, spoke to the Yale College Faculty – the first student ever to be granted that privilege – on the importance of the issues Yale was facing as May Day approached. He was articulate and impressive. Ralph Dawson, Chair of the BSAY organized the black students in a Student Marshall corps who worked with the police, New Haven community leaders, and those of us in the administration. During the May Day weekend that BSAY group was extremely important in keeping the peace.

For the first time in Yale's history we understood the importance of working closely with the city.

While we did not have the confidence of the mayor, the chief of police, James Ahern, was a close friend of mine and we shared views on what should be done. Ahern had been appointed a few years earlier by then-Mayor Richard C. Lee shortly before Lee's decision to resign the office of mayor. This decision had resulted in Bartholomew Guida, the president of the Board of Aldermen, automatically succeeding to the mayor's office. Guida kept Ahern on as Chief. Jim Ahern and I worked closely every day for weeks to keep the City's efforts and Yale's efforts on the same track.

Ahern was in his thirties and had been promoted over a number of more senior officers. He was not always popular with the force, but he was a firm leader. Both through ongoing education and by nature, he was a policeman who was in search of new policing methods. He was particularly interested in issues surrounding effective crowd control. He did not believe in "massive" police reaction to restless crowds. Rather, he used small groups of officers to separate out the people who were in the crowd just for "action" or looting, from the people who had genuine concerns. The former were individually taken in and removed from the crowd, while the latter were escorted and assisted in their protests. He used tear gas almost exclusively to end looting and similar activity and almost never to try to disperse a crowd of people with legitimate concerns.

Ahern had a wealth of contacts in the police world who educated us about radicals from other areas of the country who might come to New Haven. I had also cultivated contacts at other universities who shared information about radicals they had come across. My Harvard contact was Archibald Cox, a professor of law and aide to Harvard's president during that university's troubles. Cox became solicitor general under President Nixon and was later fired by Nixon after Cox refused to accede to Nixon's demands during the Watergate scandal. Ahern and I used the information we gained from these contacts to separate out the violent radicals from the radicals who had earnest motivations.

President Brewster and other senior administrators spent hours and hours meeting with faculty, deans, residential college masters, and students to listen to their concerns and ideas and to explain what we were trying to accomplish. While this was time-consuming, it was an extraordinarily valuable exchange of ideas and information, keeping everyone on the same track.

Brewster worked closely with the dean of Yale College, the Dean of the Graduate School and the deans of the professional schools. It was our goal to maintain the "normal expectations" for the academic calendar. Ultimately this was an area in which we failed. As we moved closer to May Day itself, the pressures on everyone became intense.
A few students and faculty – and even an administrator or two – decided that they would leave town, fearing for their safety. Some students and faculty, as a matter of conviction, turned the classes into discussions about the issue at hand, thus leaving the normal course work undone. In the end the second semester for 1969-70 was not complete. But I would suspect that many faculty and students who were here would argue that it was truly educational.

Tom Strong

York Street, near Elm, New Haven.

Finally, we were helped enormously by the work of Cyrus Vance, at that time a member of the Yale Corporation (board of trustees). In 1967 Vance had been a senior member of the Defense Department and was asked by President Johnson to go to Detroit to oversee Federal involvement in the riots that occurred there in July of that year. That report, "Final Report of Cyrus R. Vance, Special Assistant to the Secretary of Defense, Concerning the Detroit Riots, July 23 through August 7, 1967," remains an extraordinarily valuable document. Vance came to New Haven on a number of occasions as we prepared for the weekend and played a significant role in our decision-making. We implemented a number of his recommendations in our strategy.

In part with help from Vance, the Federal and State authories were convinced that Chief Ahern should be in charge of all the forces in the city during the May Day weekend. Thus he commanded not only the New Haven and Yale police forces, but also the state police and the National Guard and, though they were never brought in, the Marines stationed in Rhode Island. This prevented the kind of tragic event that occurred later at Kent State University.

We involved community leaders in all of our planning wherever possible. Almost all of the New Haven black community leaders were people with genuine concerns that needed to be addressed. Throughout the May Day period, while their rhetoric was harsh, their goals were positive. They worked with the police, with Yale, and with the Yale black students effectively and successfully.

We developed a communications program with a two-pronged effort. First, we kept everyone in New Haven and Yale informed about decisions as quickly as we could. We did not withhold information that might be inflammatory, but rather got it out and dealt with it as soon as possible. Second, we assembled the telephone numbers of key media people in case something happened in which the media would have an interest, and thus we could inform them rather than their "finding it out." This was crucial when the Yale rink was bombed, for the police radio initially indicated that there were numerous injuries and a large number of ambulances were summoned. We immediately called all our media contacts and informed them that there had been no injuries at all, merely damage to the building. This prevented a "media frenzy" which might have in turn increased crowd reactions.

Finally, Brewster urged all of us to adopt his philosophy, mentioned earlier, of treating each and every person with respect when we met with them.

Tom Strong

One of dozens of notices around Yale campus and New Haven Green.

May Day Weekend, 1970

People began to trickle in late Thursday, April 30. The major influx was during Friday, the first of May. There is no accurate estimate of the numbers, but a best guess is 20,000 to 30,000. The "visitors" seemed quite content with their housing in Yale's residential colleges. It was warm and they slept in the courtyards, eating the healthy food and using public facilities in each college.

Yale had taken over an alumni building on Temple Street as our operation center, and it had a view of the Green but was a half-block from the Green. The building had dormitories on the top two floors where off-duty University police officers could get some sleep. These were the days before cell phones and the Internet, so the telephone was the only means of good communication (walkie-talkies could be listened in on) and we had about forty phone lines installed to different areas of the campus so we could get quick information.

The night of April 30 turned out to be the most turbulent time of the weekend. The New Haven police had skirmishes with small groups who tried to break store windows, vandalize buildings, and cause minor trouble. These groups seemed unrelated to those who had come to protest the trial. Chief Ahern handled them skillfully, using effective police work and minimal tear gas.

There were two buildings damaged during the weekend: an office space, near the court house, used by the radicals was arsoned. The Yale hockey rink, which we had converted into a place for the radicals to use for a dance the night before the rally, was seriously damaged by a bomb while the radicals were in it – though happily none were hurt. It is hard to imagine that the radicals would have burned their own offices or bombed their own dance. Today we believe that this was done by associates of Attorney General Mitchell, who was so eager to have Yale fail.

The national radicals who came to New Haven met with us at 3:00 AM of May 1, the day of the rally, and we reached an agreement about who would do what and how we would keep the rally safe. Yet, in keeping with the times, the next day at the rally, President Brewster was called F------ Kingsley Brewer by radical leader who had been calling him Kingman just hours earlier in the morning.

The morning of May 1 dawned a warm, hazy day. As people moved down to the lower portion of the New Haven Green, there was an almost festive, rather than angry mood. One could see people playing the guitar, singing and dancing. Here and there an individual was giving an impassioned speech.

Behind the scenes, Chief Ahern had the National Guard between two and three blocks away from the Green and not visible from the Green. His uniformed officers moved around in groups of three or four officers, quickly stopping any untoward activity. Plainclothes New Haven and State police officers moved through the crowd, being careful not to aggravate anyone unless absolutely necessary. Tear gas was used judiciously when small groups engaged in minor vandalism, but the distant smell of it was a caution to those who might have been planning larger things.

The rally went off without a hitch; lots of rhetoric; no violence. May 2 saw a small rally of about 7,000 people and by May 3 most everyone had left town. We had not slept for a week. We all were too tired to celebrate and we are glad we did not, for a few days later four Kent State students were shot to death by National Guardsmen.

Later, Seale and the Panthers were tried and the jury was unable to reach a verdict. The prosecutors decided not to retry the case.

Three Humorous Stories

Two or three days before May Day, we asked Vance to come to New Haven and review our logistical plans. He was most complimentary of everything, with one exception. When the telephone system was explained to him he asked for a demonstration. So someone in a distant location was asked to call in. When the phone rang at the bank of forty telephones we could not tell which one was ringing and Vance smiled. He suggested we have lights on every phone!

I had learned from Archibald Cox that two bus loads of the Weathermen planned to come to New Haven for the rally. The Weathermen were, by far, the most dangerous of the national radical groups. Over the years they had destroyed buildings and murdered innocent people.

Chief Ahern and I did not want them in New Haven. After careful planning we were able to find out the bus line they were using, convinced the bus line and the police to work with us, and then prevent the Weathermen from getting to New Haven. The two buses stopped on the Massachusetts Turnpike as though there were a mechanical failure in the lead bus. The drivers got out, removed the alternators from both buses, and were immediately picked up by an unmarked police car. The disabled buses were left on the highway and the Weathermen went into the woods, never to be seen in New Haven.

We knew that the weather prediction for May Day called for very warm weather. We also knew that there might be tear gas floating around. We had window air conditioners installed in the operations building. (These were the days before universal air conditioning.) However, we neglected to adjust each unit to recycle internal air and, as the tear gas began to flow, it came right into the building, causing tears among our crew!

What Did We Learn?

University administrators found the period from the late 1960s to the early 1970s pressured, intense and, for some, educational. There were a number of presidents and their associates who just could not take the pressure and left office during, or soon after, riots on their campuses. Others were fortunate enough to make it through the period and most learned an enormous amount.

I believe there were five lessons we learned at Yale.

The first relates to President Brewster's way of dealing with people. If you go into the Grove Street Cemetery in New Haven, you will see the following quote from a speech he gave, on the wall around Brewster's grave: "The presumption of innocence is not just a legal term; rather it lies in the commonplace belief in the innocence of the stranger."

Brewster genuinely believed that each person who came to see him, who challenged him or petitioned him, had value and should be seriously listened to. The most radical person could, after conversation, find common ground with Brewster. And from this common ground compromise could almost always be found. This attitude was a far cry from the old, paternalistic, authoritarian attitude held by many college and university administrators. We found that students, in particular, were wonderful partners in keeping the peace.

Second, we learned that radical ideas are not, in and of themselves, bad. We learned to listen to them, because the radical ideas of today might well be the gospel of the future. Those who challenged authority in that period – on civil rights, on the environment, on the rights of women, on sexual orientation, and on ill-advised war – were almost always right. Their methods were harsh and unsettling, but the principles they were fighting for were valid.

Tom Strong

Third, the most difficult role of the college or university administrator is to find the fine line between allowing dissent and maintaining the ongoing activity of the academy. The primary goal of a college or university is the pursuit and dissemination of knowledge. That one principle should not be compromised. But that pursuit and dissemination requires freedom of action, thought, and speech. While the traditional pursuit of the truth on the one hand and the radical pursuit of a new truth, on the other, will at times conflict, the administrators and faculty must find a way for both to be carried on.

Fourth, many people have asked me whether the events surrounding May Day had long-term impact on Yale. With one exception, I do not think so. Yale as an institution did not change in any dramatic way. But in one sense, I do think Yale changed and for the better. When the effort to admit large numbers of minority students began, there was some skepticism both within Yale and among the alumni ranks. For some it was innate racism; for others it was reaction to change. However, during the May Day period of intense pressure and interaction the Yale minority students' extraordinary leadership eliminated the skepticism from most minds. For those of us who were not members of a minority group it was an awakening experience of real importance. The young men and women were as courageous, smart, and intelligent as anyone at Yale.

Finally, to accomplish an atmosphere in which these pressures can exist while the work of the institution goes on, people on all sides must learn to find compromise. To find compromise between parties who disagree there must be a modicum of respect. Kingman Brewster often said: "We must not allow disagreement to fester into disrespect." Thus his respect for every individual, the respect for the validity of new ideas and the ability to keep that respect healthy, proved essential.

Henry "Sam" Chauncey

31

Memorabilia, media comments,

with photographs by

John T. Hill and Tom Strong

Marcus Calls for Poll on Ouster of Brewster

Hartford – State Senate Majority Leader Edward L. Marcus today charged that "the flag of anarchy seems to be the Yale mascot" as he bitterly condemned Yale University President Kingman Brewster Jr.'s recent statement on the courts.

Marcus, a Yale graduate himself and a New Haven lawyer, proposed that a "national poll of all Yale graduates and students" be taken to determine whether Brewster should be retained as president. The Democratic lawmaker made his criticism and proposal in a two page letter to Brewster.

James Mutrie, Jr., State Capitol Reporter,
New Haven Register
April 27, 1970, page 1

Centerfold from May Day New Haven
handout (front cover shown on page 21).

The four symbolic animals are, from left to right:
bulldog, panther, alligator, and pig.
(The alligator represents the lesser-known
New Haven Underground organization.)

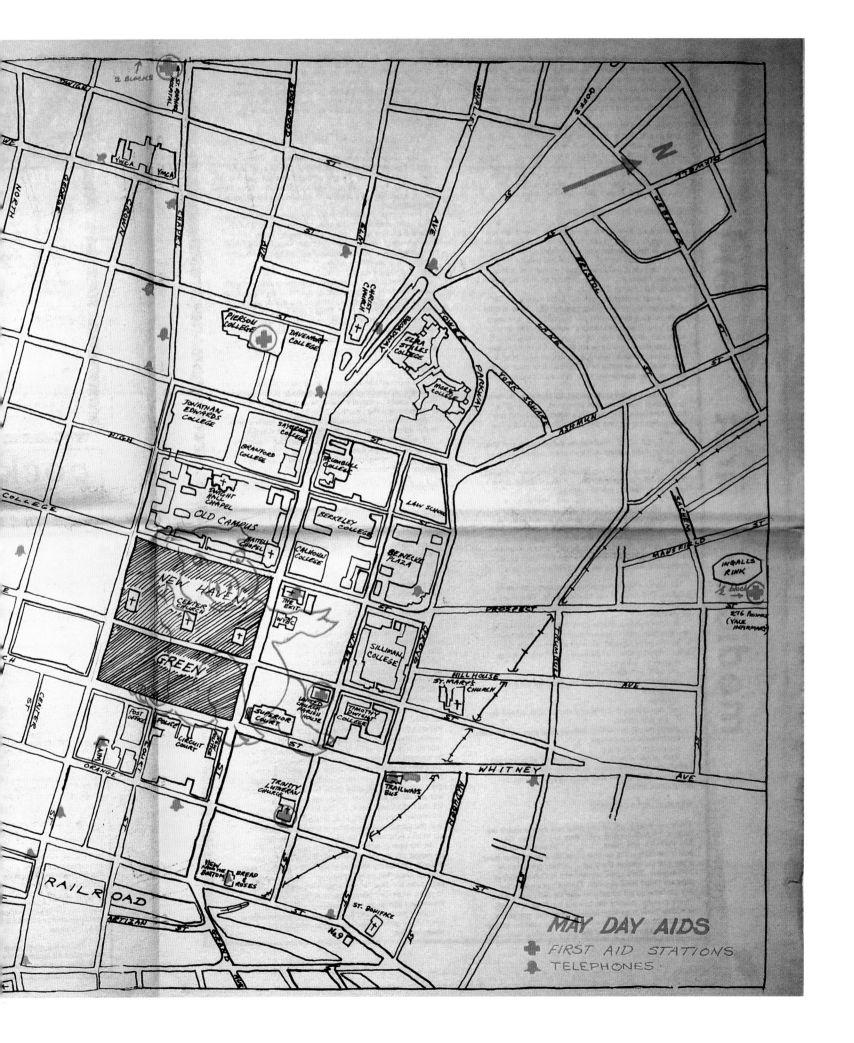

MAY DAY AIDS

✚ FIRST AID STATIONS

🌳 TELEPHONES

Peaceful Weekend Planned

By DORI ZALEZNIK and STUART ROSOW

Coordinators of the May 1 weekend have been emphasizing that they plan a nonviolent rally and have organized groups of marshals and marshals' aides this week to insure peace.

Separate statements issued by William Farley, 1970 and chairman of the strike steering committee, and by Big Man, managing editor of the Panther newspaper, declared that the rally would be "peaceful, non-violent and legal."

The steering committee statement, delivered at a morning conference attended by the national media, attacked the alleged mistreatment of the Panthers. The purpose of the demonstration, according to the statement, is to "dramatize the depth, complexity and difficulty of the contradictions that have been raised about this trial and America's relationship to it."

Ann Froines, a member of the New Haven Panther Defense Committee, said in the defense committee's afternoon conference that the rally was the first step in a chain of actions to "free Bobby and the New Haven Panthers."

At a Dwight Hall marshals meeting last night Mrs. Froines said the monitors will be persons who sympathize with the goals of the rally. She added, however, that they will be of different ages, from different communities, and of varying political affiliations.

Marshals, according to David Dixon, another Panther Defense Committee spokesman, will not act as a "miniature police force." Rather their primary function is to provide information.

The marshals, who will be identified by arm or head bands, were instructed to urge people off the street onto the green, to note information about arresting

(continued on page 3)

Committee Reports

Safety Question Rages

By SCOTT HERHOLD and JOHN COOTS

A 13-man student-faculty committee monitoring preparations for May Day demonstrations expressed skepticism last night that the activities will be as peaceful as the sponsors intend.

Concluding several days of study, the Monitoring Committee affirmed its conviction that "none of the groups involved in planning the weekend want disorder."

However, it stated the possibility for disorder in the May 1 demonstrations appears "significantly greater" than at previous demonstrations such as the October Moratorium.

The committee, which includes Yale Chaplain Rev. William Sloane Coffin Jr., Psychology Professor Kenneth Kenniston, Pierson Master John Hersey, and Kurt Schmoke, 1971, will release a complete report at a press conference today at 12:30 in Dwight Hall.

'Serious Deficiencies'

The committee noted "serious deficiencies" in the planning and organization of the demonstration:

- "Absence of precise and definite plans, agreed upon by all parties, for orderly dispersal following the demonstrations on the New Haven Green." The committee noted, "Past experience shows that possibilities for disorder are greatest at that point."
- "Absence of certainty that speakers will act consistently and decisively to discourage all incidents or to calm them should they occur."
- "Absence of a clear statement by law enforcement authorities about when and how the National Guard will be employed."
- "Incomplete provisions for a unified, coordinated, and clearly-marked organization of marshals on the Green and after the demonstrations."

The committee also raised doubts about communications between demonstrators, the local police, the state police and the National Guard. (See full statement, page 2.)

"Reports of the existence of white vigilante groups and of white radical extremists are too persistent to be ignored," the committee affirmed.

In light of its study, the group recommended "children and high school students should not attend the demonstrations in New Haven. Any other persons unaccustomed to turbulent and potentially disorderly crowd conditions should also not attend."

Response

Bill Chickering, 1970, a co-ordinator of the marshals, responded to the committee's statement by saying, "It's based on perceptions that are almost completely accurate, but lagging behind by about 24 hours."

He added, "A helluva lot can be done in 24 hours."

Chickering maintained that the committee's criticisms of crowd dispersal plans, police communications, and marshal organization were being met.

The plan for dispersal, he added, was dependent on Yale's willingness to open Phelps Gate on the Old Campus.

Chickering said the Panther Defense Committee was attempting to talk with the scheduled speakers, urging them to commit themselves to non-violence "because of the political realities in New Haven."

He said a group was meeting with the city police tomorrow in order to define the role of the marshals more exactly.

Authorities React To Demonstration

It is far from certain how city and state officials intend to respond to possible outbreaks of violence at this weekend's demonstration.

It seems likely, according to informed sources, that units of the National Guard will be deployed close to the downtown area.

New Haven police chief James Ahern has insisted privately that his forces will maintain a "low-profile" by staying out of the way of the demonstrators as much as possible.

But no one doubts that he intends to move swiftly if he feels the situation warrants it.

Two technical options seem to be open to law enforcement officials:

- they can maintain the "low-profile" image with the National Guard held in readiness, perhaps stationed within several bloacks of the Green.
- they can move in with a massive show of force, circling the Green, even before the demonstration begins.

The basic question seems to be whether a show of strength might deter or provoke a possibily unruly crowd.

Both the Kerner and Walker reports were ambiguous on this score, and in the final analysis the tactics must be determined by the size, mood and intentions of the crowd--none of which can be estimated in advance.

A lack of coordination among the state and local authorities has provided some unfortunate precedents in the past. After the last riot in Oakland, no one was able to determine who called in the National Guard.

Stephen Koch

ROBERT TRIFFIN
Cites Governance Need

Triffin Repudiates Return To Normalcy

By RICHARD M. SCHWARTZ

Yale's current crisis should leave a "positive and constructive residue" on the Yale community, according to Robert Triffin, master of Berkeley College.

"I feel it would be most unfortunate if Yale were to heave a huge sigh of relief and 'return to normalcy' after this weekend," he said.

Triffin feels that there are three areas of importance to which all members of the Yale community should turn after May 3--ensuring the Panthers a fair trial, establishing ways and means for improving Yale's relationship to New Haven, and restructuring Yale governance to allow for the effective realization of participatory democracy.

Trial Issue Neglected

The issue of achieving a just and fair trial for the Panthers has been neglected, Triffin said.

"None of the resolutions specifically dealt with the trial, and apart from statements by President Brewster and other individual faculty members, little has been said or done pertaining to the trial," he said.

Triffin feels the trial issue should be more widely discussed and last week circulated a petition concerning the trial.

The petition urged "all members of this University--students, faculty, and administration--to exert their maximum efforts and use all appropriate means at their command to help ensure the Constitutional rights of the defendants who must be presumed innocent unless and until their guilt is proven in court."

The petition collected about 500 signatures, including those of Kenneth Mills, assistant professor of philosophy, Robert Jay Lifton, professor of psychiatry, and all residential college masters.

Triffin said establishing better relations with the New Haven community is a necessary factor in Yale's re-adjustment following the present crisis.

"Yet the efforts of the entire

(continued on page 3)

First Aid Facilities Readied For Rallies

By STEPHEN LEACH

Four central first aid stations and 50 teams of medical students and undergraduates are being organized to provide medical aid, if needed, during the rallies this weekend.

In a special policy statement Dr. Charles Womer, director of Yale-New Haven Hospital, announced Tuesday no injuries except gunshot and knife wounds will be reported to the police.

He also said police interrogation of patients at Yale-New Haven will be forbidden.

Aid stations will be in Pierson College, St. Paul's Church at Chapel and Olive Streets, Trinity Lutheran Church at Orange and Wall, and the United Church Parish House at Temple and Wall, according to Dr. Jerome Grunt of the Yale Medical Center.

Dr. Grunt said each aid center will be staffed by two physicians and two nurses 24 hours a day, beginning Thursday.

The centers will be run by both Yale and community medical personel.

"These centers will provide basic first aid and help in the removal of any serious cases to hospitals," Card Ryan, a third year medical student, said.

In addition to these extra services, the Department of University Health will be open from 8:30 a.m. to 9:00 p.m. Friday and 8:30 a.m. to 5:00 p.m. Saturday to provide primarily "essential, immediate health care," according to Dr. John Hathaway, Director of DUH.

If and when the DUH facilities reach capacity, the Infirmary will become the primary medical station, he added.

Medical Teams

The 50 student medical teams will roam among the crowds and provide minor first aid treatment. If a person is seriously injured, the team will help him to one of the four aid stations.

The teams will be composed of one Yale medical student and three undergraduates. They will carry walkie-talkies to communicate with the centers.

The aid stations and teams have been jointly planned by the Medical Committee for Human Rights, (MCHR), the May Day Coordinating Committee and the Yale Medical Center.

The MCHR is an organization of medical personnel formed to provide medical assistance at civil rights demonstrations, according to Dr. Ellis Perlswig, president of the local MCHR chapter.

"Yale Infirmary, as well as the stations, will be available to anyone," Dr. Grunt said.

Comfort Stations

Comfort stations are planned for most of the residential colleges, according to Miss Ryan. Though they will essentially be places in which to rest, pairs of medical students will probably be on hand in each college.

She also said a transportation group is being formed in case ambulances are needed but unavailable. No ambulances will be kept at the aid stations.

Miss Ryan emphasized that all medical personnel will take a completely neutral political stance during the demonstrations.

Dodd Asks Senate To Investigate Rally

By JOHN GEESMAN

United States Senator Thomas Dodd, in a televised statement yesterday, called upon the Senate Judiciary Committee to make a full investigation of the events leading up to the demonstrations planned for this weekend in New Haven.

Dodd said he has "information and evidence that clearly indicts the administration and some of the students of Yale who have been led into the position of helping a national conspiracy to wreck the legal process.

"The press has reported the theft of 500 riot guns and rifles in the New Haven area and some fires of suspicious origin, but there are other things that have not been reported.

"I know, for example, that over 5,000 rounds of ammunition were purchased in Massachusetts this morning by a Black Panther official from New Haven," Dodd said.

He also claimed that "a large group of radicals who have been in Cuba cutting sugar cane for Castro, and now back in Canada, are on their way to New Haven."

Dodd charged that there have been inflammatory fliers distributed "in the name of the so-called defense committees, and I have some in my possession."

There have been calls for violence this weekend, he said, "including the killing of the so-called pigs."

"All of this is of concern to me as a Senator from Connecticut," Dodd concluded, "and I am asking the Senate Judiciary Committee to make a full investigation of this entire terrible situation."

The Senate Judiciary Committee is chaired by Senator James Eastland, a Democrat from Mississippi.

Dodd's press secretary said that Dodd's Juvenile Delinquency Subcommittee of the Judiciary Committee might possibly conduct the investigation.

2500 Students At Mass Meeting Hear Pleas For Continued Strike

Stephen Koch

Douglas Miranda, area captain of the black Panthers, spoke before 2500 people last night in Ingalls Rink. Miranda claimed police were harassing the Black Panther headquarters in New Haven and said he had heard "on good authority" that police planned to shut down the headquarters.

Non-Violence Emphasized

By WILLIAM BULKELEY

Approximately 2500 students attended a mass rally in Ingalls Rink last night to hear plans for May Day and a discussion of the Steering Committee demands.

The most repeated themes were the importance of keeping May Day weekend non-violent and the urgency of continuing the strike after May 4.

The meeting, which was chaired by William Farley and Kurt Schmoke, both 1971, featured John Froines of the Chicago conspiracy, Doug Miranda, area captain of the Black Panthers, and Kenneth Mills, assistant professor of philosophy.

The meeting began with a threat of dissension contained in a petition circulated to most of the crowd. The letter asked people to "demand open discussion tonight."

Petition Defeated

Schmoke read the petition to the crowd and explained there would be open discussion at the end of the meeting. A vote was taken on the petition and it was overwhelmingly defeated.

Schmoke opened the meeting by criticizing Vice-President Spiro Agnew's attack on Kingman Brewster and read a letter from Yale Corporation member William Horowitz which decried Agnew's attack. Schmoke also read a petition which he said would be circulated today, calling for Agnew's resignation.

Horowitz's letter and the proposed petition both received thunderous applause.

Mills received the greatest applause of the evening. Discussing the importance of continuing the strike after the weekend, Mills said, "We aren't going back. We want to see justice done, we intend to see justice done." Over half the audience rose to applaud Mills.

'Free Bobby'

Mills said, "There is one clear and simple demand--that is, free Bobby, free the Panthers." He warned earlier, "We are not going to tolerate the lynching of the Panthers in New Haven."

He urged the audience to "forget your semantic distinctions on the demands and start dealing with the issues."

Froines, the first speaker of the evening, dealt with the question of violence during the weekend. He said he felt "tension in New Haven. I don't understand the tension when people are afraid of their own brothers and sisters," he said.

He said he was delivering a message from the Conspiracy: "On Friday, Saturday and Sunday we want a peaceful demonstration." He said the chief aim of the May Day weekend was to "help free Bobby," and he added a peaceful demonstration is the only way to do it.

"Until Bobby Seale is freed, the strike cannot end here," he added.

Miranda Speaks

Douglas Miranda claimed the

(continued on page 3)

Brewster

Controversy Intensifies

By RICHARD FUCHS

The controversy surrounding Kingman Brewster Jr. intensified yesterday as Connecticut Governor John Dempsey attacked the Yale president, and Trustee William Horowitz, Law School Dean Louis Pollak, and over 3000 Yale students rose to his defense.

The 3000 students signed a petition supporting "the leadership of President Kingman Brewster during the past few weeks," and John Cole, 1971, initiator of the petition, presented it to him in Beinecke Plaza yesterday afternoon at 4.

Horowitz

Earlier yesterday, Horowitz, a member of the Yale Corporation and chairman of the Connecticut State Board of Education, released the text of a letter he sent to Vice President Spiro Agnew.

Tuesday night Agnew had called for the removal of Brewster as Yale's president. Horowitz termed that request "unjustified, irresponsible, and self-serving."

He said, "It is perfectly clear that your Florida speech is a continuation of your systematic campaign to inflame popular passions against anyone dealing constructively with the problems confronting American society today."

The letter continued, "Your blatant disregard for facts which inconveniently contradict your prejudices is unworthy of the office you hold and the nation you claim to serve.

"I frankly do not believe that your experience as a president of a PTA chapter qualifies you to evaluate the contributions to education by the most distinguished university president in the United States."

Horowitz went on to commend Brewster's handling of the present crisis and lauded his efforts "to strengthen the dual cause of non-violence and freedom of expression."

He also said Mayor Bart Guida, Police Chief James Ahern, and Judge Harold Mulvey are "dealing responsibly with the situation."

Dempsey

Governor Dempsey disagreed with Horowitz's analysis.

Referring to the Yale president's statement that he was "skeptical of the ability of black revolutionaries to achieve a fair trial anywhere in the United States," Dempsey said, "The statement he issued shocked me, as I think it shocked a lot of other people in this state."

When asked if he agreed with Agnew that Brewster should resign, the governor said that decision should be left to Brewster's conscience.

Yale Corporation member and New York Mayor John Lindsay disagreed with Dempsey. He condemned Agnew's "intemperate language" on the New Haven situation in a speech at the University of Pennsylvania last night.

Pollak

Dean Pollak took issue with Agnew's statement, maintaining that "it could mean one of two

(continued on page 3)

Yale Studies Needs Of Incoming Crowd

By MICHAEL SHERMAN

Yale will attempt to provide food for all the demonstrators this weekend and housing for as many persons as the fire laws allow.

Since estimates of the number of visitors coming to New Haven range from 8,000 to 30,000, administration officials are hesitant to devise a final housing plan.

"We'll be flexible and we'll try to accommodate all that we possibly can--either in the colleges or other university facilities," said one administration source.

Unofficially, the number of persons which can be housed in the colleges and Old Campus is 8,000, in addition to undergraduates already in residence.

A rotation system will be used which will allow all the demonstrators to be fed, Director of Dining Halls Albert Dobie said yesterday.

Dining facilities will be set up in the courtyards of each college and on the Old Campus.

Officials plan to feed 35,000 persons for each of two meals on Friday; 25,000 for each of two meals on Saturday; and 10,000 for the Sunday meals.

"Student marshals will attempt to regulate the flow of traffic into each college so that the number of people eating at any one time in a courtyard does not exceed the number housed in the college," Dobie explained.

Gerald Swords, secretary of the Council of Masters which participated in the decision, indicated it would be difficult "to count noses."

Thus, students will redirect marchers to other courtyards or to the Old Campus when a college becomes too crowded for comfort.

Representatives from the Student Steering Committee spoke to the Council of Masters' meeting yesterday and urged the University to endorse a completely "open-door" policy in housing the demonstrators.

Mike Petru, 1973, recommended that Yale utilize all available space including classrooms to accommodate everybody needing a place to sleep Friday and Saturday nights.

No formal request has yet been made by the steering committee to the University, according to Alfred Fitt, advisor to President Kingman Brewster Jr. He added, "Anyway, a classroom's use is not compatible with sleeping."

Most of the students who addressed the Council stressed the importance of Yale making the visitors feel welcome.

"Our principle problem is to keep the visitors happy," said one Steering Committee mem-

(continued on page 3)

Stephen Koch

Representatives of the national media flooded the hockey rink last night. The national media came in for heavy fire from several of the speakers who said the strike at Yale was being misrepresented.

Yale Daily News

On April 30, law student Richard Balzer displays an armband to be worn
by legal observers to help maintain order at the rally.

United Press Telephoto, Photographer unknown, Courtesy of the Joe Taylor Collection

Tom Strong

Yale Art and Architecture Building,
corner of Chapel and York Streets.

Tom Strong

Chester Kerr, director of Yale University Press,

on bicycle near the Yale Art and Architecture Building.

Tom Strong

Tom Strong

Gentree Ltd., York Street adjacent
to the Yale Art and Architecture Building.

The text written on the plywood reads:
"Free the Panthers!"
"We demand immortality"
"The February 35th Movement"
"Freakology"

Professor John Hersey, beside National Guard jeep,
across the street from the Yale Art and Architecture Building
Thursday afternoon, the day before May Day.

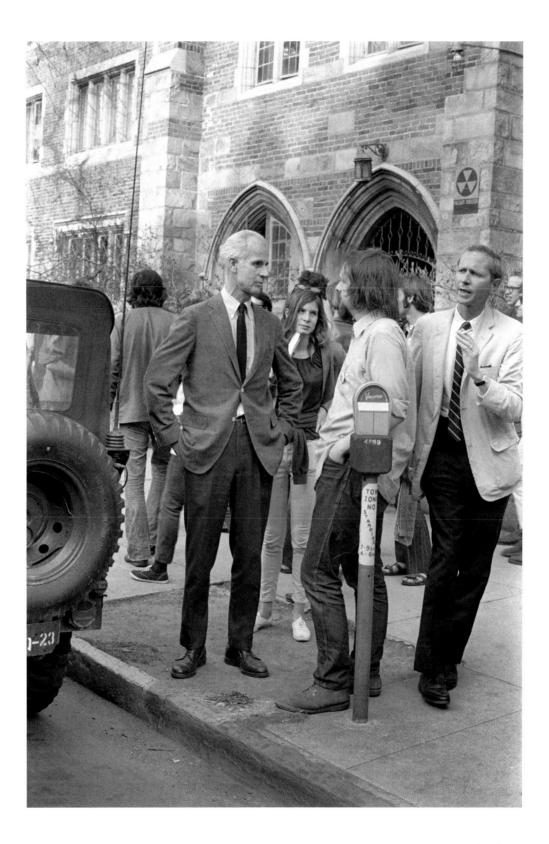

Tom Strong

Guard Arrives to Aid Police

What seems certain to be the largest political demonstration in New Haven's history began today on the city's historic Green.

Organizers expect between 20,000 and 30,000 demonstrators, as well as several thousand National Guardsmen, an undisclosed number of State Police and the city's 425 man police force. In addition, 4000 Marines and Army paratroopers have been moved to military bases in Rhode Island and Massachusetts as a precautionary measure. They will be brought to New Haven if needed.

Despite intricate and myriad precautions to prevent violence, the city was nervous.

Francis J. Whalen, assistant city editor, and Sam Negri, staff reporter, *New Haven Register*
May 1, 1970, page 1

State Street near Corner of Chapel Street

While the mass of demonstrators did not notice them until last night, the National Guard surfaced in New Haven yesterday afternoon a few blocks from the Green.

Hidden in the complex of governmental buildings near the site of the demonstration were forces of the State Police as well. The Guard was deployed at 3:45 yesterday afternoon, in areas near the Green. Although no forces were within view of the demonstration, large groups of Guardsmen were stationed around the city.

Three main contingents formed the brunt of the deployed force. One group numbering about a hundred stationed itself on York Street, across from the Davenport-Pierson College area. A second large force was reportedly stationed in the vicinity of the Grove Street Cemetery. This contingent was also said to number one hundred, according to eyewitnesses. The third major Guard forces are part of the Task Force Bravo, the designation for all troops standing by in the New Haven area.

Lewis Schwartz and Thomas Kent, *Yale Daily News*,
May 2, 1970

John T. Hill

Broadway on May Day morning

A painted red rifle with the words "In the spirit of CHE!" referring to Che Guevara, appearing on the plywood protecting Cutler's window.

Tom Strong

Tom Strong

Broadway on May Day morning.
opposite: Blue Jay Cleaners, Broadway

Tom Strong

Common Reason Must Prevail

An explosive situation is brewing in New Haven over the impending Black Panther murder trial and the times call for an immediate lowering of the heat and cooling off of passions. Outside influences have invaded the City and are weaning, cajoling and haranguing – with intemperate, spiteful rhetoric – the Yale community and the City's own high school population into acts of protest that can serve no purpose but to disrupt the City's normal life and its climate of calm and order.... The threatening situation now boiling in the City must be brought to a halt. Voices of calm and reason must come forward and be heard loud and clear.

Editorial, *New Haven Register*, Thursday, April 23, 1970, page 16

Shoppers, Employees Staying Home
Many Downtown Businesses Forced To Close

Business today was clobbered by the Black Panther rally,
as thousands of shoppers and workers avoided coming
into New Haven. Many stores and offices and some factories
are closed because of the fear of disorder. All stores in
the Chapel Square Mall, the "showcase" of the downtown
retailing area, are closed.

The Greater New Haven Chamber of Commerce had
recommended that stores and other businesses remain
open, but this is being widely ignored.

Walter Dudar, business editor, *New Haven Register,*
Friday, May 1, 1970, page 45

opposite:

Liggett's, on the northwest corner of Broadway and York.

The text written on the plywood reads:

"General Accident Insurance has cancelled our policy."

"We're off to the rally!" "Free the Panthers!"

Tom Strong

Tom Strong

Entrance to Pierson College on York Street.
The gentleman in coat, tie, hat, with cigarette,
at left, is a Yale Campus policeman.

*Pierson established one of the main first aid centers in its common
room. The staff of doctors, medical students, and nurses treated over
thirty cases, all for minor injuries. One of the earliest cases was an
allergic reaction to the peanuts in the Familia.*

Sam Swartz and Greg Fullerton, *Yale Daily News,* May 2, 1970

Tom Strong

Entrance to Davenport College on York Street. Hand-painted signs on a sheet that was put up before the rally.

Davenport set up a family and child day-care center, which handled about two dozen youngsters. Several undergraduates played babysitter all day with the tots, who ranged in age from a few months to six years.

Sam Swartz and Greg Fullerton, *Yale Daily News,* May 2, 1970

52

Saybrook College wall, corner of Elm and Park Streets, looking south.

Tom Strong

Yale Daily News May 1, 1970

Rally To Launch May Day Weekend; 25,000 Expected On Green Today

Brewster Statement At News Conference Defends 'Skepticism'

By RICHARD FUCHS

Yale President Kingman Brewster Jr. outlined his position on the events leading up to this May Day weekend at a press conference yesterday morning at 11.

Speaking before about 50 representatives of the national news media, Brewster emphasized the "common objectives shared by all members of the Yale community--the promotion of legal and social justice."

Referring to today's planned gathering on the green, he said, "This is not a Yale rally; it was not organized by a Yale group."

Brewster maintained that relatively few members of the Yale community had urged that the trial of Bobby Seale and eight other Black Panthers for the murder of Alex Fackley be stopped, but he stressed Yale's concern that justice be done in the case.

"No Woodstock"

"This is no picnic. This is no Woodstock," the Yale president continued. "Probably some who want violence will be here."

Brewster said he and most other members of the Yale community wanted to see a peaceful demonstration. He said violence would greatly harm the cause of the Black Panthers on trial here.

"Innocence is no protection if violence breaks out," he added.

He indicated Yale's role in housing and feeding those who come to New Haven this weekend was designed to help insure the preservation of the non-violent nature of the demonstrations.

"Opening up the University would be a much smaller provocation than keeping all the gates closed and retreating into a fortress," Brewster added.

He said he was "immensely proud of the energy, common sense and good will of the Yale community" displayed throughout the past few weeks.

Asked about Vice President Spiro Agnew's call for his ouster as Yale's president, Brewster said, "I'm not going to make any response to the Vice President."

Skepticism

Several reporters challenged Brewster on his statement issued last Thursday that he was "skeptical of the ability of black revolutionaries to achieve a fair trial anywhere in the United States."

He said he had not intended to disparage the legal system or any of its judges by his statement.

"The question of the fairness of a trial is not limited to the motivation of the judge, but it extends also to the political atmosphere in which the trial is held," he added.

A trial involving revolutionaries, and especially black revolutionaries, is bound to create a great deal of political passion--sufficient passion to justify an expression of skepticism about the possibility of a fair trial, Brewster said.

Questioned about the propriety of his statement, Brewster emphasized that he had made it in a private capacity, and not as a representative of Yale University. He said he would not retract the statement or alter its wording.

He stressed the University's concern with legal and social justice, "with particular relation to Yale's role in the community."

He denied reports that the student strike had polarized the community, saying there was a widespread belief in the "common objectives" of all members of the community.

"The only differences are those of means and degree," he added.

Brewster denied reports that he was planning to resign as a result of the present crisis.

Hoffman, Dellinger To Speak

By MICHAEL SHERMAN and CHUCK CRITCHLOW

Yale administration officials said yesterday they expect only 9 to 12 thousand people needing a place to sleep over the weekend.

They therefore foresee no difficulties in following President Brewster's directive issued earlier this week which permits colleges and the Old Campus to house guests "up to the limit of sensible and safe housing."

The upper limit of "sensibility" would be approximately 13,000 persons including current boarders.

The Fire Marshal recommended this limit after conducting a survey of all the colleges and the Old Campus.

"The question of a fire law is not involved," said Henry Chauncey, Jr., Special Assistant to the President. "The Fire Marshall came up with a sane and sensible figure. If individual colleges want to be insane and insensible by exceeding the limit, it's up to them--I won't know about it."

No Student Steering Committee request for the use of other University facilities such as classrroms or Ingalls Rink was ever received by the administration, Chauncey added.

If additional space is needed to house visitors, the New Haven Green will be available, according to police sources.

Mike Petrau, 1973, coordinator of the Student Housing Committee, indicated that one to two thousand persons can be accomodated in area homes and churches. He hopes, however, to house all visitors on the Yale campus.

University officials plan to keep the main gates at each college open throughout the weekend.

At least one campus policeman will be stationed at this gate at all times.

Whether secondary gates remain open will be the decision of the members of each college.

Chauncey said, "The main gates will be closed in only two circumstances: if I order them closed, or if the officer at the gate believes there is a real clear and sudden danger for the people inside the college."

University officials declined comment on whether Phelps Gate would remain open.

Although Yale plans to house only 9000 visitors, it will provide food for over 35,000 demonstrators, most of whom are expected to be from the New Haven area.

The Department of Dining Halls has over-extended its credit by $8,000 as a result of having to buy such large quantities of food this weekend, according to a member of the student food committee.

The University hopes to cover this cost with "non-coercive donations" from diners, contributions from college social fees, and the regular weekend operating budget for board.

Larry Engel

Supplies and army communications equipment are stocked in the basement of the Hall of Records. The building is located behind City Hall.

Larry Engel

Fears of violence were expressed by many yesterday. Tags for shirts, posters screaming "Violence is the tool of fascism" and boarded-up windows appeared across the campus and around New Haven.

Preparations For Guests Completed

By WILLIAM BULKELEY

No one was sure whether they were preparing for a "Woodstock Nation," or a "Days of Rage," but preparations for the expected Mayday weekend influx were made all over the campus yesterday.

Estimates as to the size of the expected crowd varied. Bill Farley, 1971, and chairman of the Strike Steering Committee, said 15,000 to 25,000 were expected but added he felt only about 10,000 will stay at Yale tonight.

Today, Mayday, will see a rally from 4 to 8 on the lower Green. David Dellinger and Abbie Hoffman of the Conspiracy will speak. Other speakers include Carol Brightman of the Venceremos Brigade and Big Man, assistant Minister of Information of the Black Panther Party.

The food committee announced it expected to feed 25,000 to 35,000 people at supper today. People will be fed out of doors at all the colleges and on the Old Campus.

Last night the housing committee reported "lots of people" have already come to them and asked for housing. Housing is available in every college.

Today is the main rally for the three day weekend.

The main rally will be followed by more speeches at Yale and dances on the Old Campus and at Ingalls Rink.

It will be preceded by a 10:30 press conference at the Courthouse.

Most of Saturday will be devoted to workshops on a wide range of subjects. These groups will meet at Yale from 10-12 in the morning and from 2-4 in the afternoon.

An afternoon rally on the Green will follow the workshops. Speaking at the rally will be Artie Seale, wife of Panther Chairman Bobby Seale, Tom Hayden, John Froines, Jerry Rubin and other members of the Conspiracy, the French playwright Jean Genet and Ralph Abernathy of the Southern Christian Leadership Conference.

After 8, demonstrators will move back to the campus for dances at Ingalls Rink and on the Old Campus.

Sunday, a Black Music Festival will take place, probably on the Yale campus.

Medical Plans

Medical stations have been set up in Pierson College, at the

(contined on page 4)

National Guard To Patrol Streets; Federal Troops Held In Reserve

Governor Calls Guard

By JOHN COOTS

Police Chief James Ahern announced yesterday morning that National Guard soldiers "will be deployed throughout the city to supplement local efforts" of the New Haven police patrols.

The statement followed an announcement yesterday by Governor John N. Dempsey saying the National Guard would be deployed in New Haven and federal troops would be in readiness this weekend.

Dempsey acted on a formal request for assistance from Mayor Bart Guida. The troops have been ordered on duty as of 9 this morning.

Indications are the soldiers will be deployed on the main arteries leading to the Green and in neighborhood areas outlying the campus.

The National Guard has established a field headquarters in the basement of 200 Orange Street.

Ahern said the additional manpower of the Guard "will enable the City to do all it can to insure an orderly and non-violent demonstration and permit the city to function as normally as possible."

Whether the city will function normally is doubtful. Shops on the periphery of the Green are being boarded up as though

(continued on page 4)

Weekend Schedule

Friday, May 1
10:30 am.: Press conference in front of courthouse with representatives of participating organizations
12-4 pm.: Rock music on the Green
4-7: Main Rally on the Green. Speakers include Abbie Hoffman, Dave Dellinger of the Chicago 8; Carol Brightman of Venceremos Brigade; Big Man of Black Panther Party.
7-2am. (longer if possible): Dancing plus speeches at Ingalls Rink. Old Campus, other areas to be announced.

Saturday, May 2
10-12n.: Workshops on complete range of subjects.
2-4: Locations to be announced; contact Peter Countryman at Dwight Hall for information or suggestions.
4-8: Rally on Green. Artie Seale, Black Panther Party. Tom Hayden, John Froines of Chicago 8. Jean Genet, Ralph Abernathy, plus others to be announced.
8- : Music etc. Locations to be announced.

Sunday, May 3
3 pm.: Black music festival. Locations to be announced.

Mitchell Calls 4000 Troops

Four thousand federal troops were dispatched yesterday to bases in New England at the request of Connecticut Governor John Dempsey.

Dempsey asked for the troops in a telegram as "precautionary measure" in the event that police and National Guard are unable to contain the potential violence in New Haven this weekend.

The 4000 troops are drawn from the 2nd brigade of the 82nd Airborne Division, stationed at Fort Bragg, North Carolina and from the 1st regiment of the second Marine division stationed at Camp LeJeune, North Carolina.

The paratroopers have flown to Westover Air Force Base in Chicopee Falls, Massachusetts, about 70 miles from New Haven; the Marines were sent to Quonset Point Naval Air Station in Rhode Island, about a two hour drive from the city.

The troops can be deployed in New Haven only by executive order of President Nixon. Dempsey, however, requested the troops "pursuant to a subsequent request for their use and assistance."

Government sources reported that Nixon "informally" approved of the transfer of the troops and possible use of the troops but has not ordered their deployment.

The justice department said yesterday that a "civil disturbance team" headed by Assistant Attorney General William Ruckelshaus is in New Haven to observe the rally.

Dempsey, in his telegram to Mitchell, justified the request for troops, saying that "based on present information it is further my opinion and that of the attorney-general of the State of Connecticut that the local and State police forces, supplemented by the National Guard, if totally committed, should be able to contain any violence that might occur.

"However, there remains a strong possibility that the violence might escalate beyond our capacity and that additional forces would be necessary," he continued.

Nixon, according to the White House spokesman, echoed Dempsey's belief in approving the troops and said there was no reason to believe that the units would be used.

"We are confident that a successful effort on the part of local authorities, students and administrators at Yale will keep the demonstration peaceful," the government source said.

Yale Faculty Denounces Cambodian Involvement

The newly revealed policy of the Nixon administration toward Cambodia was criticized yesterday by a number of Yale faculty members.

The consensus was expressed by H. Bradford Westerfield, professor of political science, who said, "The Nixon administration is running very grave and unnecessary risks in expanding the war.

"My own strong feeling is that we were better off with Sihanouk. We should have joined with North Vietnam in reimposing him on the country. Then he would be indebted to both us and the North Vietnamese.

"The reason for this is I think he's going to win, and win with only the communists supporting him."

Asked about the present stance of the Senate Foreign Relations Committee, which has opposed further involvement, Westerfield said,

"It's highly desirable. The administration is moving in the opposite direction of where we should be going. I believe we're over-extended in defending all of South Vietnam. I don't believe this should be broadened to other countries."

Scully's Nightmare

Vincent Scully, master of Morse College, called the Cambodia policy a "nightmare."

"It's the same thing all over again," he said.

"The thing that frightens me most is that the Pentagon seems to be taking the matter into its own hands. It's getting to the point where the Pentagon seems to be the real enemy. They are growing more uncontrolled.

Isaac Kramnick, assistant professor of political science, said, "The entire affair is disgusting. We've been here before. The whole thing is a typically Kissengeresque plan."

Asked about the effect of the intervention on domestic politics, Kramnick replied, "I don't think Nixon can win against a unified Democratic Party in 1972 if he gets us involved in Cambodia."

On the role of the CIA, he said, "I would be very surprised if the CIA hadn't played a large role in the overthrow of Sihanouk."

After the announcement by President Nixon last night that the US was sending several thousand American troops into Cambodia to pursue the North Vietnamese, Westerfield had these further comments: "He's escalating both the war and the rhetoric."

'Gross Distortions'

"The speech was filled with gross distortions. Never did he mention the overthrow of Sihanouk, or even the existence of Sihanouk. Nor did he point out the extremely likely contingency that the North Vietnamese will simply withdraw deeper into Cambodia, dragging us in after them.

"Nixon is grasping at straws. More and more, he sounds like Johnson in the last year-and-a-half of his Presidency.

"The best solution to me," continued Westerfield, "is to let Thieu's control shrink to an area large enough to accommodate those South Vietnamese who are not Communist. Then he could control without the United States backing him up."

Wesleyan Struck By Bombings

A series of fire bombings and a bomb scare shook Wesleyan University yesterday, hours before a rally there in support of the New Haven Panthers.

A police investigation so far has uncovered no suspects or clear motives in the incidents.

Early yesterday morning half of a music annex on the Middletown, Conn., campus was destroyed by fire. A student store also was damaged when a fire bomb was thrown in one of its windows.

Between 4:30 and 5:30 yesterday morning three false alarms were turned in on campus. Shortly after those alarms, the interior of a building being converted to a data processing center was gutted by flames.

At 6, an undetonated Molotov cocktail was found in another music annex, and at 11 a bomb scare occurred at the University's science center.

No persons were hurt in the fires.

Last night, a mass rally at the University heard members of the Black Panther Party and John Froines, a Chicago 9 defendant. Campus police and 350 student volunteers planned a special fire watch to guard against further incidents.

One Wesleyan secretary took her files home with her last night in fear her office would be burned, according to sources at Wesleyan.

Media's Multitudes Mass In Elm City

By LEW SCHWARTZ

"My mother didn't want me to come down," said Bice Clemow, owner of the Hamden Chronicle and the West Hartford News. "But I couldn't resist it," said the longtime newspaperman.

The elite of the press corps, well over a hundred strong, has descended on New Haven in anticipation of disturbances relating to the May Day demonstration.

Reporters represent papers that range from the Washington Post to the Los Angeles Times. All the New York papers and the three television networks are strongly represented.

"I just wish there was some place to eat in this hole," said one reporter, who has suffered the ordeal of life in the Elm City since Tuesday.

But for most of the journalists and TV commentators the week has been both educational and reminiscent of their college careers.

Woodstock Notion

"This is a beautiful thing to watch happen," NBC's Lem Tucker said of the Yale scene. The flashy dressing broadcaster spent over five minutes describing the New Haven situation on the Huntley-Brinkley Report with Charles Quinn, last night.

Tucker and Quinn form the main contingent of a 25-man NBC crew now in New Haven.

"This is a major story," Quinn added. "I only wish there were more people already here."

The two NBC men toured the Yale campus this evening, trading jibes with Branford students and Dwight Hall workers.

After wandering into a Branford Bach Society meeting, Tucker said, "They aren't the people I love, but they sure sing well."

Competing With Cambodia

All of the major networks and news magazines are represented in the throng. Both Time and Newsweek are considering this as a potential cover story. "Its only competition is Cambodia," said Time's Greg Wierzynski.

"We are Yale-oriented here," the national educational correspondent added. "There is an interesting juxtaposition between what's happening on the Yale campus and on the Green. We realize that this is a new thing for Yale."

The Connecticut press corps is also here in force. Ed Chinnock of the Hartford Times focused his feature on the Yale student.

"I'm really interested in the reasons why students have chosen this time to make a stand." The correspondent features one student in a column for today's paper.

Generally, the massed minions of the media are waiting for today and tomorrow. "It's a big story," one executive said.

Larry Engel

Mellow Yellow

Student Marshals will wear yellow headbands to identify themselves. These marshals are responsible for giving information and directions.

Yale News

Old Campus with portable toilets, before the rally.

New Haven Green, before the rally.

John T. Hill

Tom Strong

New Haven Green, northwest corner of Temple and Elm, early afternoon, May Day.

Tom Strong

Northwest corner of Elm and Temple, early May Day afternoon.

Among the banners carried to the rally on May Day were:

Free the Panthers
Women's Liberation
Stop Racist Attacks on Panthers
Unemploy [Kingman] Brewster
Compensate Workers
Fight Ruling Class Attacks on Black People
Killing Animals Creates Killing of Men
Smash racist ROTC
U.S. out of Trinidad and S.E. Asia

Tom Strong

Tom Strong

The New Haven Green across from City Hall (above and at right).

John T. Hill

Allen Ginsberg, second from the left, and

Kenneth Mills, assistant professor of philosophy at Yale, right of center.

Tom Strong

Seated in center: Artie Seale and Michael Tabor. Composite photograph.

John T. Hill

Allen Ginsberg, Jerry Rubin, and Abbie Hoffman.　　　*John T. Hill*

Yippie leader Jerry Rubin kicked off the May Day "Free Bobby Seale" demonstration with a rousing two-hour monologue that drew yells, foot-stomping, and raised fists from two-thirds of an audience of 1600 in Woolsey Hall early yesterday afternoon. Rubin, a charter member of the Chicago Conspiracy, declared that all schools were "concentration camps" and urged that "Yale University be closed down forever." "The most oppressed people in America are white middle class youth," he said. "Yale students are more oppressed than children in the ghetto, who are fighting for revolution. Yale students are fighting to protect only the b-------."

He described Yale as "a racist place where they separate the rich from the poor. Yale is a criminal place because here rich white America has declared war on the black and the poor." Rubin asserted that "a fair trial for Bobby Seale is totally impossible because the laws of this country are to protect property and therefore automatically oppress black people." "If Bobby Seale, not Teddy Kennedy, had been driving the car that went over the bridge with Mary Jo Kopechne," said Rubin, "he would have been lynched."

Jeffrey Gordon, *Yale Daily News*, May 2, 1970

Over 20,000 Expected At May 1 Start

The Chicago Conspiracy Seven, Attorney William Kunstler, the Rev. Ralph Abernathy, and a crowd estimated by rally supporters at from 20,000 to 30,000 persons will arrive in New Haven next week for three days of demonstrations, beginning May 1, in connection with the Black Panther trial here.

The major events planned for the demonstrations are a mass rally on the New Haven Green from 4 to 8 p.m. on Friday, May 1, and a "summing–up" rally on Yale's Old Campus Saturday afternoon, according to Peter Countryman, a spokesman for the Black Panther Defense Committee, which is co–ordinating the plan.

Stanley Fisher, Jr., staff reporter,
New Haven **Register**, April, 24, 1970, page 1

Although the crowd was docile at the rally which started at 4:00 p.m., May 1,
the speeches it heard were not.

John T. Hill

John T. Hill

Four main points were repeated in the speeches: the necessity of freeing Bobby Seale

the pervasiveness of the U.S. policy of
imperialism and racism against both the people
of Southeast Asia and the blacks in this country

the need for continuation of the struggle against
the government after this weekend until
"the people finally win"

the need for non-violence this weekend
because the time was not right for violent revolution

Michael Sherman, *Yale Daily News*, May 2, 1970

Jerry Rubin was born in 1938. He dropped out of Berkeley and joined the left-wing radical movement, opposing the Vietnam war, supporting black movements and the legalization of marijuana. He joined the "Yippie" movement and was the foremost advocate, among radicals, of using modern communication methods to promote radical causes. He appeared before the House Un-American Activities Committee of the Congress dressed as an American Revolutionary radical!

John T. Hill

Chicago Defendants Vow Non-Violence - But Insist Panthers Must Be Freed

Standing beneath flags emblematic of the "Legalize Marijuana" movement, the Chicago Conspiracy Eight, minus one, opened the May Day rally with speeches before a crowd of newsmen and demonstrators elbow-to-elbow in the Center Church on the Green today.

Phrased in revolutionary rhetoric, the Conspiracy announced an enduring commitment to work for the freedom of Black Panther Bobby Seale and other Panthers through non-violent means, a commitment which begins actively today.

Lights from still and television cameras flashed on Abbie Hoffman, Jerry Rubin, John Froines, David Dellinger, Rene Davis, Thomas Hayden and Peter Weiner of the Conspiracy Eight and David Hilliard and Elbert "Big Man" Howard of the Black Panther party as they addressed the throng.

Froines opened the conference by introducing the speakers and asserting that the "Conspiracy will come back here again and again until all nine (Panthers being held for trial here) are free."

John T. Hill

Jerry Rubin, dressed in red pants and a multi-colored "tie-dyed" shirt with the "Legalize Marijuana" flag hung cape-like from his shoulders, opened the conference by announcing that one reason for coming to New Haven was to "destroy the concept of the Conspiracy Seven," declaring that they should be called the Conspiracy Eight to include Bobby Seale. "Just because that racist Judge (Julius) Hoffman has put him in jail doesn't mean that Bobby Seale isn't part of the Conspiracy. Anyone who calls us the Conspiracy Seven is a racist."

Rubin promised that the Conspiracy is not "going to rest, to sleep until Seale is free" and asserted that the police raid on Black Panther headquarters in Baltimore, Md. Thursday is "an attack on all of us."

Speaking next, "Big Man" also referred to the reported raid, charging that police have made this town an armed camp, and in Baltimore they moved to establish another conspiracy and murder. He claimed that search warrants "give the pigs the right to kick down the doors of our offices and our homes … in attempts by pigs to annihilate our leadership and the entire Black Panther party."

Stanley Fisher, Jr., staff reporter, *New Haven Register*, May 1, 1970, page 1

John T. Hill

John T. Hill

"Abbie" Hoffman was born in 1936 and was a co-founder of the Youth International Party, or the "Yippies." He participated with many of the radical leaders, including Seale, Hayden, Hoffman, and Rubin, in the violent protests of the 1968 Democratic National Convention.

John T. Hill

John T. Hill

John T. Hill

John T. Hill

John T. Hill

John T. Hill

Tom Hayden, born in 1939, was arguably the most important radical leader of this period. He was a "freedom rider" in the south; president of Students for a Democratic Society (SDS); drafted the Port Huron manifesto, which rejected bureaucracy and authority; violated the law by going to North Vietnam during that war; and took his radicalism into politics as a member of the California State legislature. He has been called "father to the largest mass protests in American history."

Born in 1910, Jean Genet started life as a vagrant and petty criminal, but was best known as playwright, poet, and essayist. His works were provocative and challenging. In the late 1960s he became active in politics in France, the U.S., and the Middle East. The Black Panthers invited him to the U.S. in 1970. He was an intellectual leader of the radical movement worldwide.

Elbert Howard, "Big Man," served as translator for Jean Genet He was also a key figure in the Panther organization.

82

John T. Hill

John T. Hill

John T. Hill

John T. Hill

John T. Hill

Kenneth Mills, assistant professor of philosophy at Yale.

John T. Hill

88

John T. Hill

"Artie" Seale, the first wife of Bobby Seale, and Michael Tabor.

John T. Hill

"Artie" Seale was a strong member of the Black Panther Party. She actively supported her husband and maintained a full-time job at the same time. Her income provided funds for much of the beginning of that movement, including their first guns for defense. She is said to be writing a book about these experiences.

John T. Hill

John T. Hill

John T. Hill

Peace in the Air

Just prior to the start of Saturday's rally, a sky writer left a peace sign over New Haven Green. Tweed New Haven Airport had no record of this flight. The tower controller reported the incident to the New York control center.

New Haven Register
May 2, 1970, page 9

John T. Hill

John T. Hill

John T. Hill

John T. Hill

His Own Crusade

It was was essentially a rally in support of the Black Panthers, but other causes were represented. This man seems to be crusading for a universal vegetarian diet.

New Haven Register
May 2, 1970, page 5.

John T. Hill

John T. Hill

John T. Hill

John T. Hill

John T. Hill

John T. Hill

POLITICAL PRISON
OF U.S.A. FASCISM

John T. Hill

Richard Balzer, Yale law student. According to FBI records Balzer was the official photographer for the Black Panther Party.

John T. Hill

Paul Helmle, Yale architecture faculty.

Tom Strong

NATIONAL
BLACK
BUSINESS SHOW
SPONSORED BY THE EBONY BUSINESSMEN'S LEAGUE
MAY 8-9-10 1970
STATE ARMORY HARTFORD, CONN.

John T. Hill

John T. Hill

John T. Hill

John T. Hill

John T. Hill

National Guard on Elm Street near corner of Church Street.

Photographer unknown, Courtesy of the Joe Taylor Collection

New Haven police chief, James Ahern.

Fire gutted the New Politics building, corner of Elm and Church, Saturday night.

Photographer unknown, Courtesy of the Joe Taylor Collection

Yale Daily News May 2, 1970

Evening Outbursts Follow Peaceful Rally

Assistant Professor of Philosophy Kenneth Mills addresses the crowd of approximately 10,000 on the Green yesterday afternoon. Mills, a leader of the Yale Strike, told the gathering that our society is racist and must be changed. Larry Engel

Demonstrators, Police Engage In Skirmishes On Tear-Gassed Green

By TOM WARREN

Confrontations between rock-throwing demonstrators and New Haven police erupted late last night after false reports of arrests drew an angry crowd of demonstrators to the Green.

The police resorted to tear gas on several occasions in an attempt to contain the crowd, and National Guardsmen were utilized to seal off the campus for several hours late in the evening.

An uneasy truce finally prevailed early this morning as the demonstrators withdrew into the campus for the night.

The police reported 17 demonstrators arrested during the series of brief skirmishes, and five persons were treated for minor lacerations, according to a spokesman at the Yale-New Haven hospital.

The incidents last night were the first to mar the May Day organizers' hopes for non-violence. A bombing at Ingalls Rink late in the evening caused some destruction but only three minor injuries.

To The Green

The confrontation on the Green was touched off by a speaker who took the microphone from Jerry Rubin at a workshop in Branford College to announce that "several brothers" had been arrested for going on the Green after dark.

The speaker, who claimed to be a Black Panther, elicited chants of "To the Green" from his listeners.

Rubin reportedly spoke to advise against such an action, but was unable to convince the crowd not to march to the Green.

Similar announcements, reportedly made at Abbie Hoffman's workshop in Stiles College and at a band concert on the Old Campus, drew an eventual crowd of over 1000 to the Green.

Led by standard-bearers of a Boston-based group known as Youth Against War and Fascism, the group marched around the lower edge of the Green and was directed back toward Phelps Gate by student marshals.

As it reached the Gate, however, the crowd abruptly swung back toward Chapel Street with cries of "To the streets" and marched to York Street before the marshals could turn it back toward the campus.

At Elm Street, the marchers turned toward the Green again, and all the efforts of the marshals to turn them into High Street were to no avail.

Confrontation

The crowd finally halted at the corner of Church and Elm on the lower corner of the Green, and the marshals linked arms to bar any further progress. Facing the group of demonstrators across Church Street were police and Guardsmen directed by Chief James Ahern.

The small group of marshals proved unable to disperse the demonstrators, and at 10:25 several rocks and a stink bomb were thrown from the crowd at the police.

Ahern then responded by ordering tear gas to drive the crowd back from Church Street.

For the next hour there were occasional flare-ups as the Yale marshals attempted to herd the demonstrators back onto the Old Campus, while the police and Guard units manned the periphery of the Green.

Tear Gas

When small groups of demonstrators engaged the police by throwing rocks and bottles, they were met by tear gas, first at the corner of Temple and Chapel Streets and then at the corner of College and Chapel.

A small but powerful explosion shook a dwindling crowd at Ingall's Rink last night, causing three injuries and some damage to the front of the building.

Police reported that three small bombs went off simultaneously at midnight in the right front stairwell of the rink. The crowd of approximately 75 filed out of the building immediately, ending a rock concert by the Eschaton, a band from the Berkeley Divinity School.

According to observers, one man was hospitalized for smoke inhalation, and two girls were treated for cuts. None of the casualties were serious.

The police had no immediate leads on who might have planted the bomb, which scattered glass 80 feet in front of the rink.

In the latter incident the police used a more potent tear gas, believed to be of the CS variety, to drive the remaining demonstrators onto the Old Campus. By this time, many of the policemen had removed their badges.

Following the incidents on the Green a group of Guardsmen cordoned off York Street at the corner of Chapel and were confronted by a small crowd. When the crowd failed to disperse, the Guardsmen fixed bayonets.

Eventually, however, they were persuaded by a group of Yale marshals which included Chaplain William Sloane Coffin to withdraw to the far side of Chapel Street.

Although the identity of the speaker at the Branford meeting is still uncertain, there is some doubt that he was actually a Panther. Doug Miranda, New England Panther area captain, took the microphone on the Old Campus at 11 last night to announce that the reported arrests had not occurred, and Panther members worked with Yale marshals throughout the evening in an attempt to control the crowd.

In the early hours of the morning Ahern announced that the National Guard was being withdrawn, except for a detachment of about 400 soldiers on motorized patrol.

EDITORS FOR THIS ISSUE
News: John Coots
Business: Doug Garrison
Photography: Larry Engel, Stephen Koch
Copy Editors: Rich Fuchs, Bill Bulkeley, Nick Perensovich
Night Editors: Lew Schwartz, Phillip Cheron, Alan Beller

The National Guard was called in to back up the New Haven Police Force last night. The Police used pepper gas to disperse the crowd. Later, the Guard was used to seal off the Yale campus, bringing about an uneasy truce late last night. Stephen Koch

Quiet Afternoon

Rally Hits Racism

By MICHAEL SHERMAN

The rally held on the Green yesterday afternoon gave little indication of what was to occur later in the evening.

Approximately 10,000 people gathered in what seemed to be a lazy spring afternoon mood to hear speeches and dance to the tune of several rock groups who performed as people sauntered into the area.

Prior to the beginning the planned rally, SDS held a mini-meeting opposite the New Haven City Hall. Over 700 persons gathered to hear speeches denouncing racism and oppression of workers in this country, while the band played on.

The mini-rally ended after twenty minutes, and the SDSers rejoined the main crowd without incident.

Speeches

Although the crowd was docile at the rally which started at 4, the speeches it heard were not.

Four main points were repeated in the speeches:

- the necessity of freeing Bobby Seale,
- the pervasiveness of the US policy of imperialism and racism against both the people of Southeast Asia and the Blacks in this country,
- the need for continuation of the struggle against the government after this weekend until "the people finally win," and
- the need for non-violence this weekend because the time was not right for violent revolution.

David Dellinger of the Chicago Conspiracy called on thousands to converge on Washington, D.C., next weekend to force the government to end exploitation of American "colonies" at home and abroad.

Other speakers at the rally included David Hilliard, chief of staff of the Black Panther Party; Kenneth Mills, assistant professor of philosophy at Yale; Abbie Hoffman of the Chicago Conspiracy; and French Author Jean Genet.

Big Man, minister of information for the Panthers, began the rally by reading an open letter from Genet, who later addressed the crowd in French since he speaks little English.

Genet told American students that the time may be at hand when they will have to "desert the universities and leave the classrooms to carry the word across America about the racism in this country."

This met with loud applause from the audience, composed mostly of college students.

Black Oppression

The situation of black people was stressed often throughout the afternoon.

Mills, in primarily addressing the white students, said, "We are in a fight for every single oppressed individual in the world today.

"This racist society corrupts you. How many people are free in this society? You much understand racism, because it is killing you. You too are oppressed whether you recognize it or not."

In an earlier speech, Hilliard said, "We will put our finger on the trigger and show the Attorney-General we'll do whatever is necessary to end tyranny against Black People in this country. We'll do anything because of our condition."

No one--from the administration to liberal politicians--was immune from verbal attack.

"The liberals have once again stated, as they have done all through history," shouted Robert Shear of Berkeley, Calif., "that if institutions they find comfortable and satisfactory are challenged, they will turn to fascism rather than give up power."

Though all the speakers asked for non-violence this weekend, they felt violence would have to be the eventual answer.

"Fascism begins at home and the administration is out to devour us. So fuck-off you philistines from Washington," Hoffman said.

There's no course but to the streets with this system we've got," he continued. "If they find Bobby guilty, we're going to pick the fucking building up (the courthouse) and send it to the moon."

Yale's Role

Mills and Hilliard both stressed more than any of the speakers the need to continue the struggle and Yale's role in it.

"It's an important precedent when Yale University stands up for justice for Black people," said Hilliard. "I think this is an example all students and colleges should follow."

Mills said, "We struggled to close Yale down in order to open it up to reality. The struggle has only begun."

"We said at Yale" the Black Panther repression "cannot go on, must not go on, and is not going to go on."

At 6:15, the persons who had gathered on the Green began to disperse with a minimum of commotion.

A Yale student marshal saw a friend and clasped his hands together and smiled optimistically because the rally had been peaceful.

His optimism was short lived.

Black Areas Stay Cool, Expect Continued Peace

By STUART ROSOW

Spanish-speaking and Black community leaders were relieved as last night's disturbances and demonstrators were confined to the downtown area.,

Fearful of potential damage to their communities, a group of Black and Spanish community leaders issued a statement at yesterday's press conference calling for peaceful protest this weekend.

"As the silent majority reactionaries arm themselves in panic, as irrational white crazies contemplate destroying this demonstration, as white hoodlums threaten to invade our neighborhoods, as local police refuse to legitimize our efforts to peacefully help prevent provocative situations, as federal troops and the national guard-trained and not so trained-killers-mobilize around us...we Black and Spanish speaking people can plainly see the threat to our survival," the statement read.

Coordination

Responding to this threat, the Black and Spanish Community Control Network, a group coordinating the efforts of numerous community organizations, groups and churches, has established a "community patrol to limit violence upon our people."

The role of the patrols will be to monitor the neighborhoods in the Hill and provide guidance for people attending the rally, according to the statement.

Though the leaders stressed non-violence, they voiced strong support for the Panthers and the rally.

Don Ogilvie, who read the statement, is chairman of the "School Volunteers", an educational self-help organization. He said last night that he was pleased that the rally "went as smoothly as it did."

"Waiting Game"

He described the situation in the Hill as a "waiting game" for whatever might happen, and reiterated his hope that the weekend be "as quiet as possible."

Black leaders felt the primary source of potential violence in their neighborhoods this weekend was provocation by police forces.

Ogilvie enumerated the police and the National Guard as the two organizations which would be "responsible for trouble.""

Fred Harris, community advocate at the Connecticut Mental Health Clinic, said the community was "mad as hell," about the presence of the National Guard. Harris added that the community would have to protect itself from the police danger.

Margaret Leslie, a neighborhood organizer at Newhallville, called the National Guard "trigger-happy uptight cops."

She also attacked those who are leaving New Haven for the weekend, saying they were "abdicating their responsibility to the community."

She included in her attack Yale students who have left campus while she had praise for those students who were remaining to participate in the demonstration and for those who were working for better relations between the University and the Black community.

Intimidation

Elaborating on her comments about police and national guard, she charged that the law enforcement agencies' show of force was a "manifestation of intimidation of Black people."

Though the community was "concerned" about the increased presence of police forces, Mrs. Leslie said she discerned no fear in the neighborhoods and said "whatever happens will be all right."

Marcus Ocasio-secretary director of the Junta of Progressive Action, said he expected no trouble in the Spanish community this weekend since the use of the Guard "was not a surprise."

Ocasio also stressed the role of the community patrols in keeping the people calm.

Another Puerto Rican leader, Pedro Ramierez, said the mood of the community was to "sit tight and see what the police are going to do." He said if there was no provocation by police the community would remain quiet this weekend.

Schedule and Info

Saturday, May 2

10-12n: Workshops on complete range of subjects.

2-4: Locations to be announced: contact Peter Countryman at Dwight Hall for information or suggestions.

4-8: Rally on Green. Artie Seale, Black Panther Party, Tom Hayden, John Froines of Chicago 8, Jean Genet, Ralph Abernathy, plus others to be announced.

8 - Music etc. Locations to be announced.

Sunday, May 3

3 pm: Black music festival. Locations to be announced.

Information

EMERGENCY TELEPHONE NUMBERS

Campus Police	436-4400
Fire	436-8341
Ambulance	787-4141
Health Aid Station	562-1161
24-Hour Emergency Repair Service	436-8081
Legal Assistance	436-1106
Housing	436-0110
Davenport Day Care Center	436-3062
May Day Committee	436-0115

Yale Daily News

Courtesy of Avco Embassy Picture Corp.

Photographer unknown

Cover and lead articles
designed by
Hiram N. Ash
MFA, Graphic Design
Yale Art and Architecture, 1960

Photography unknown,
courtesy of the Joe Taylor Collection

Polara

Those notes, the chords, that melody...

It's Bacharach . . .

I travel to childhood,

I've landed in the back of the "Polara"

I crank down the window . . .

The sky is bluer than I realized,

I see the familiar heads in the front seat,

Yes they lead the way, Mom, Dad . . .

Traveling through the sixties with their kids,

I know I'm being sheltered . . .

I hear the sounds of Vietnam . . .

Dr. King? Why? Who did that?

Robert Kennedy? He was John's brother . . .

"Where we goin' Ma?"

"Uncle Al's for a few days"

"Why Ma? Why can't we stay home?"

"They say there may be riots,"

"What is riots Ma, what are they?"

"People are unhappy, they want everyone to know."

"Hey Dad, think we can swim in Uncle Al's pool?"

"Don't you always Joey?"

"Yeh, guess I do . . . you mean it's ok to have fun during the riots?"

"Sure it won't change things . . . "

"OK Dad . . . what do you think will change things . . . ? "

Joseph James

1-1-09

Like many New Haven families,

the parents of this ten-year-old poet-to-be col-

lected their young and left to visit friends—

away from the chaos that was expected for

May Day.

This is a another firsthand recollection.

Acknowledgments

This complex and worthy project could only have been taken on with the passion and dedication of a multitude. Some were unborn in 1970 and for a few, it is vivid still. For all, it seemed not a job, but a meaningful work that deserved their best efforts.

Our first thanks goes to those who gave their time, encouragement, and advice. They provided the vital tangibles and the rare intangibles. Alphabetically, they are: Richard Balzer, Turner Brooks, Tom Carey, David Dickson, Corinne Forti , Nathan Garland, Richard Nash Gould, Dorothy O. Hill, Robert Lisak, Charles Negaro, James Righter, William Schubart, Mark Simon, Robert A.M. Stern, Barry Svigals, Jeremy Wood, and Robert Yudell.

We thank Walker Drew Strong for the disovery and selection of articles in the *New Haven Register* from April 1970.

George W. Edwards was our trusted consultant regarding Black Panther Party history.

Joe Taylor contibuted key images from his trove of historical New Haven ephemera.

David Wilk, Yale 1972, offered his editing, production, and publishing skills. He was standing on the Green, May 1, 1970.

Copy editing and fact checking were done by Judith Schiff, John Wilkinson, David Baker, and Steve Wasserman.

The initial book design was produced by Margaret Watkins and Laszlo Feher. In a benign daylight heist J.T. Hill took their design and made changes with the counsel and consent of its originators. Separations were produced by Hill.
The final book reflects their collective efforts.

Unless noted, all printed ephemera is from the collection of Tom Strong.

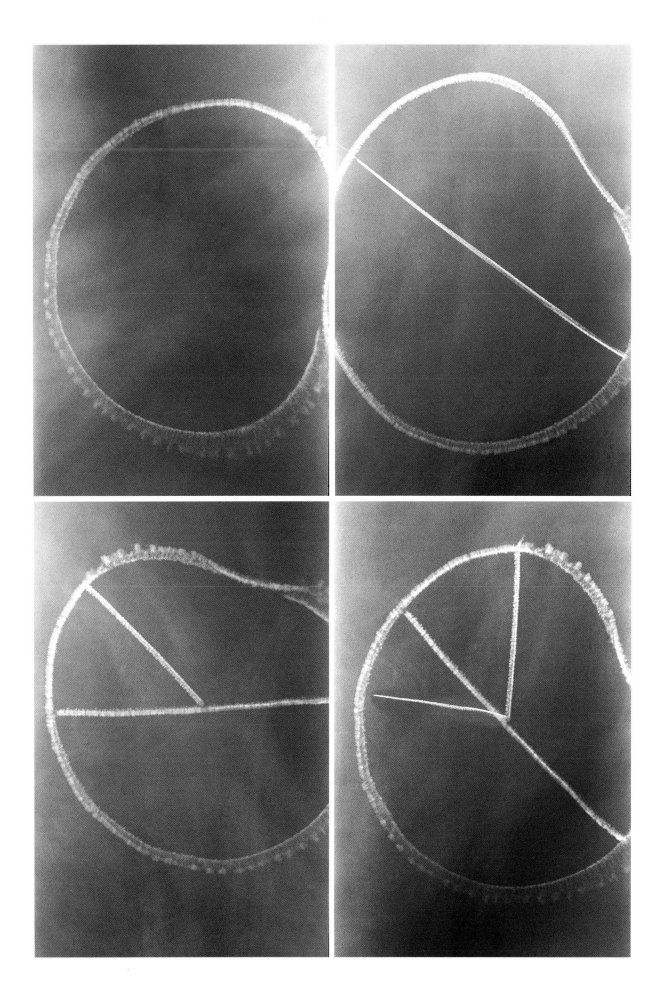

Tom Strong

Henry Louis Gates, Jr., known as "Skip," was born in 1950. He graduated from Yale University in 1973. Emmy Award-winning filmmaker, literary scholar, journalist, cultural critic, and institution builder, Professor Gates has authored seventeen books and created fourteen documentary films and film series. The recipient of fifty-three honorary degrees and numerous prizes, Professor Gates was a member of the first class awarded "genius grants" by the MacArthur Foundation in 1981, and in 1998, he became the first African American scholar to be awarded the National Humanities Medal. The founding director of the Hutchins Center for African & African American Research and the Alphonse Fletcher University Professor at Harvard University, he resides in Cambridge, Massachusetts.

Photo by Marjorie Cone Gordon

Thomas Strong was born in 1938 in Hanover, New Hampshire. He was graduated from Dartmouth College in 1960. From 1960 to 1963 he served with the U.S. Army Security Agency in Europe and in Turkey. In 1971, he was graduated from the Yale School of Art and Architecture, with a degree in graphic design. Walker Evans was his principle instructor in photography. Since 1968 he and Marjorie C. Gordon have directed the design firm Strong Cohen on Chapel Street in New Haven.

Henry Chauncey, Jr, known as "Sam," was born in 1935. He graduated from Yale College in 1957. He worked in various administrative capacities at Yale from 1957 to 1982. He then was founding CEO of Science Park Development Corporation in New Haven; subsequently President and CEO of Gaylord Hospital in Wallingford, Connecticut, and finally Lecturer and Head of the Health Management Program in the Yale School of Public Health. He is retired and resides in New Haven.

Photo by Sven Martson

John T. Hill was born in 1934. In 1955, he received a BFA; in 1956, an MFA, both from the University of Georgia. After two years in the U.S. Infantry he came to the Yale School of Art and Architecture, receiving a MFA in graphic design 1960. He taught there for 19 years, becoming its first director of graduate studies in photography. In 1975, on the death of his friend Walker Evans, he became executor of that estate. On leaving Yale, he has designed and authored various books and exhibitions.